CROSSES OF THE PEAK DISTRICT

Neville T. Sharpe

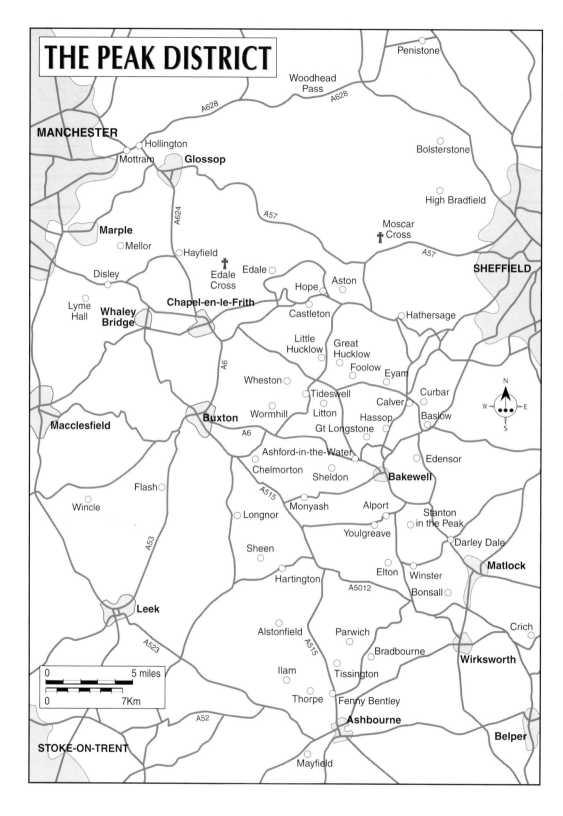

CROSSES OF THE PEAK DISTRICT

Neville T. Sharpe

Published by

Landmark Publishing Ltd
Ashbourne Hall, Cokayne Ave, Ashbourne, Derbyshire DE6 1EJ England
Tel: (01335) 347349 Fax: (01335) 347303
e-mail: landmark@clara.net
web site: www.landmarkpublishing.co.uk

ISBN 1 84306 019 1

Print: Bookcraft, Midsomer Norton
Design: Mark Titterton
Cover by James Allsopp

Front cover: The Butter Cross, Basford, Cheddleton, Leek (photograph by R. Scholes)

Back cover top left: Eyam; **Middle:** Ilam (photograph by C.L.M. Porter); **Right:** Wheston (photograph by
C.L.M. Porter); **Botttom:** Great Longstone market cross

Page 1: The 'Battle Cross', Ilam (photograph by C.L.M. Porter)

Title page: Cross in Bakewell Churchyard from *Chantrey's Peak Scenery*

Photograph Credits: All Photographs by the Author except where Indicated

CONTENTS

Maps

PREFACE

The idea for this brief survey of Christian crosses came from an article in the magazine of the Sheffield Clarion Walkers, written by the editor and founder, George Herbert Bridges Ward. It started as a few notes on crosses in the area and has been growing steadily over a period of several years until details of almost two hundred crosses, ancient and modern were collected. Information has been culled from a variety of sources; handbooks published by churches; local histories; articles in archaeological journals; a study of old maps and articles and of course intelligence gathered from farmers and others when walking over the area.

Jack Wrigley taking a break on Kinder Scout

It is by no means a complete list and it is always possible that some other old cross, or parts thereof, may be discovered when new building work takes place. At the same time it may prove worthwhile to make a list of what exists at present, since at any moment antiquities are being lost by theft, vandalism and official indifference.

The illustrations consist mainly of photographs and drawings made from photographs taken by myself in recent years with the exceptions of the photograph of Glossop Market Cross which is just one of the many taken by my grandfather T W Sharpe at the end of the nineteenth and beginning of the twentieth centuries; the photograph of the New Cross near Bradfield which was taken by Mr. Terry Howard of Sheffield; and several others provided by Mr. Barry Shaw of Penistone, Lindsey Porter and Ron Scholes.

I would like to dedicate this book to my good friend Jack Wrigley who died on Brown Hill in July 1996 whilst on an expedition in search of antiquities. Much of what little I know about ancient artifacts I learned in his company. He had an uncanny ability to spot anything the least out of the ordinary as we walked along some footpath. Without a word he would point to some tiny object underfoot and further examination often revealed a chipping of flint or a petrified hazelnut.

I will always remember an occasion when he pointed at a stone in a dry stone wall. At a first glance it looked like any other stone in the wall, until Jack said: "Take a look at the other side."

Sure enough the stone passed right through the wall. Suddenly daylight dawned, its cross-section suggested that it had once been a mullion in some long demolished building. A further examination of the wall revealed a couple more stones of the same shape.

"They wouldn't have carried them far," announced Jack, and a search of the field behind the wall soon revealed a mound which looked as if it might have once been the site of a cottage. Just to add weight to such a theory, there was a patch of nettles on the spot. A few minutes scratching at the soil with a stick and the discovery of a few pottery fragments, which looked distinctly Victorian, plus some well rusted hand made nails made it seem still more likely. It seemed that wherever we went, Jack would spot something of interest that most people would have passed by without a second glance It might be a portion of an ancient cross built into a wall; the remains of an old mill weir or leat; the site of a medieval beacon, or even a fossilised leaf on a piece of shale. When out walking, I often think of our expeditions together and marvel at his remarkable powers of observation and knowledge of the subject.

Neville T. Sharpe
January 2002
PERTH, Western Australia

1 INTRODUCTION

Walking around the various corners of Peakland towns and villages, in churchyards, or along old tracks, sometimes where they coincide with parish or township boundaries, one may come across a part of our history and a reminder of early English Christianity in the shape of the remnants of a stone cross. The area under consideration is fortunate in that it contains some of the finest examples of carved Saxon crosses and dozens of comparatively plain crosses of which, in most cases, only the base or base and stump remain. Some of these are considered as worthy of indication on the Ordnance Survey maps, others fail to warrant inclusion. This immediately poses the question, what goes on a map, and what is omitted? A market cross in the centre of a town may well be omitted because there is insufficient space to insert a symbol whereas a lone cross at the summit of some lonely moorland track may be honoured by inclusion in a suitably old script.

With every revision of the map, a decision has to be made as to which new features are to be included and which old ones have to go. For example, on maps at the end of the 19th century the site of Charlesworth Cross was clearly marked whereas modern maps make no mention of what once must have been a prominent landmark. On the other hand Hollins and Martinside Crosses are still marked although you would have great difficulty in finding any trace of them.

Every cross is not marked by any means, and if you keep your eyes open you may find portions buried in field walls or incorporated in religious buildings. Local stone varies in its workability and hence we find that in the limestone country crosses and door jambs and lintels are often made from millstone grit brought from some distance. Bearing this in mind and the fact that a piece of sandstone incorporated in a limestone wall stands out clearly, a different piece of stone in a wall should be given more than a cursory examination. Every piece of sandstone set in a limestone wall may not be part of an ancient cross but it could well be a mullion, lintel, or slopstone from some long demolished cottage, each piece with a story to tell.

Almost all of the roadside and boundary crosses in the region are mutilated, and generally, only the base and perhaps the stump of the shaft remain. The reasons for the ruined state of many of these crosses are varied. Some of the deterioration can be put down to fair wear and tear by the elements especially where crosses have been exposed at high points on moorland tracks for perhaps more than a thousand years. More recently this damage has been accelerated by the effects of acid rain and it might be a wise course of action if some of the better preserved crosses were placed inside buildings.

In a paper entitled: '*On the Pre-Norman Sculptured Stones of Derbyshire*', published in the *Derbyshire Archaeological Journal* in 1886 by the Rev. G. F. Browne appears the following comment about which very little has been done in the intervening 116 years;

> "*It too often happens that those who have the custody of stones of this character, even when they recognise that they are of priceless value from their great age, the skill of their design and execution, and the fact that no other nation in Europe has such memorials, are disposed to argue that what has lasted so well for ten or eleven hundred years will stand the weather for any number of years more. They forget that the fragments have been carefully preserved in the soil of the North Anglian or Mercian churchyard,*

and in the cement of the Norman church wall, for all these centuries, and that they will perish like any other stone in this smoky nineteenth century. It is beyond the power of words to express the folly of leaving such gems as the Ilkley shafts to perish as they are perishing."

Most of the damage, however, was deliberate; for instance, the removal and defacing of images was ordered by Edward VI in 1548 during the religious upheavals of the time. Robert Parkyn, the curate of Adwick-le-Street in Yorkshire noted that in 1548:

"Rogacion Days no procession was made about the feildes, butt cruell tirranttes did cast down all crosses standing in open ways dispittefully."

Almost a hundred years later, in 1643, during the English Civil Wars, an Act of Parliament was passed ordering the removal and destruction of crosses in public places and all representations of any angel or saint in any parish church were to be taken away, defaced and utterly demolished. Various churches were despoiled, the stained glass windows were smashed, fonts taken into fields to serve as cattle troughs, altar slabs used as bar counters in public houses etc.

It is difficult after the passage of a few hundred years to understand why there should have been such enthusiasm for wrecking inanimate objects which were often works of art. In medieval times it was customary for the owners of estates to assign a portion of the rent or often a portion of the estate itself to a religious foundation. The effect of this over a period of time was that an enormous proportion of the nation's property was in the hands of the church, even in Saxon times. This wealth attracted the attention of several kings before Henry VIII dispossessed the monasteries, but there must have been an undercurrent of dissatisfaction among a large section of the population. Here we have the makings of the stories of Robin Hood taking purses from fat abbots and distributing the proceeds among the poor.

Wyclif and the Lollards must have given the bishops at the end of the 14th century a shock which they transmitted to those who succeeded them during the next 100 years. Lollardy might have been suppressed, but their ideas must have been current for years afterwards and been absorbed into Protestantism in later years. There are similarities between the enthusiasm for overthrowing and breaking crosses and the eager way in which statues of Stalin were toppled from their plinths in more recent times.

The mutilation and destruction of many crosses must surely have caused distress to folks who regarded them as an important part of their lives. It is easy to understand why some were discreetly moved and hidden away until a change in government might make it safe to re-erect them. It was certainly no help to those who relied on them as way markers over desolate moors.

Inside churches, murals were covered in whitewash, religious statues were overthrown and shattered, but the recumbent figures of former landowners and their ladies were usually left unmolested since they were not regarded as symbols of Popery, and in any case they were often the ancestors of the Lord of the Manor of the day who might well make his presence felt. In addition to the antics of religious bigots, there have always been those lacking in intellect who cannot leave the handiwork of others alone; vacuous youths have always been with us.

More recently when commons and moors were enclosed for agricultural purposes and for grouse moors, crosses were thrown down, and in some cases buried, on the instructions of landowners in an effort to hide clear indications of ancient rights of way.

Before the English Civil Wars, Charles the First had been engaged in various schemes to increase the royal revenues and among these was the enclosure of Crown land and wastes which could be sold or leased. The limits of these enclosures were marked out by landmarks such as streams, prominent rocks, thorn trees and of course, ancient crosses. The folks who had gained the use of this land would almost certainly take advantage of the upheavals during the war to add some extra acres to their holdings. After all they had the examples of the leadership on both sides of the conflict who were adding to their own wealth whenever the opportunity arose. Later, in 1673, the Bailiff of the High Peak, Richard Shallcross, asked for a report on the wastes and commons which had been enclosed or were in the process of being enclosed before the outbreak of hostilities. From the Crown's point of view this survey revealed a sorry state of affairs with many of the boundary marks having disappeared. It requires no quantum leap of the imagination to hazard a guess at who was responsible.

Early during World War II a number of stone guide posts were buried as part of a policy of removing all signs to prevent spies and parachutists finding their way about the country. Whether it had the desired result is a moot point, it certainly caused considerable inconvenience to residents. Some were dug up again and replaced later, often incorrectly, but it is easy to imagine that in some cases their whereabouts were completely forgotten. A similar state of affairs must have occurred earlier with the village and wayside crosses and now we will never know just how many of them have disappeared for ever. However, they have a happy knack of turning up from time to time when one is unearthed as part of a building project, or change in use of agricultural land.

From 'Highways and Byways in the Border' by Andrew and John Lang, 1913, comes yet another example of cross destruction and the motives for it:

"Over in Teviotdale, too, the same passion for altering, or for sweeping away relics of old times, ran its course. In 1762, the Town Council of Hawick gave orders for the destruction of the Town's Cross. So Popish a thing as a Cross could not be tolerated by these worthy and 'unco' pious persons. The treasurer's accounts of the time show that tenpence per day was paid to two men for the work of taking down the cross, and the carved stones seem to have been sold afterwards for eleven shillings and sixpence. No doubt the worthy bailies congratulated themselves on having not only rid the town of an emblem of Popery, but on having made quite a handsome monetary profit over the transaction."

This is by no means an exhaustive list of the ways in which crosses can be lost to us; we shall come across others later as we examine the locations and types of crosses.

The great majority of the crosses in the region can be classified as boundary or wayside crosses. In many cases they serve both purposes. The next sizeable group are those standing in churchyards, but many of these are either market or boundary crosses moved there for safe keeping.

When placed by roadsides and on hill-tops they were intended to call the thoughts of the passer-by to a sense of religion; doing duty as boundary markers, guide posts, or landmarks at the same time. They were also placed along roads to parish churches used for processions. They are found in various parts of England on difficult old bridle ways and in exposed situations; for example in the area, we have, or once had, Whibbersley Cross, and the Lady Crosses, plus the Charlesworth, and Edale Crosses.

As boundary posts, crosses may have defined the limits of certain monastic or other areas, holdings, or shootings, etc., and acted as sanctuaries of various sorts for both men and animals. The Lady Cross at the summit of the Woodhead Pass for instance, marks the bounds of the lands of the Abbots of Basingwerke. They were also used in old charters to delineate the boundaries of the lands of Kings and Lords. Edale cross stands at the junction of the three wards of the Forest of Peak. Records dating back to Saxon times relating to boundaries are few and far between for the area under consideration but in one, King Athelstan ordered that the boundaries of Beverley be marked by four "nobly-carved" stone crosses.

When located inside buildings, at the entrance to churches, or on memorials or tombs, crosses were intended to inspire a sense of reverence. They were invariably devotional when placed there during the pre-Reformation period, and, today, the fourteen stations of the cross, in Roman Catholic churches, mark the progress of Christ from Pilate's house to Mount Calvary.

Pope Gregory the Great sent Augustine and forty companions on a mission to convert the heathen English to Christianity. The party landed in Thanet in early AD 597 and were fortunate in that the Kentish King Aethelberht, had married Bertha, daughter of Charibert, the Frankish King reigning at Paris, at some date prior to 588. It is reasonable to assume that Christian practices were followed within the king's household during the years before Augustine's arrival since the Frankish Bishop Liudhard had accompanied the queen to Britain.

Legend has it that Aethelberht, afraid of the stranger's magic insisted on meeting Augustine and his companions under the open sky. The interview served to convince him of their honesty and as a result he gave them a dwelling place in Canterbury, supplied them with food, and allowed them to preach their religion. At first Aethelberht refused to abandon his own pagan beliefs which were held by all the English, but he was eventually won over and accepted Christianity.

I would imagine that when the missionaries first came to convert the Anglo-Saxons they would carry the cross as a symbol of their faith and that simple wooden crosses would be erected along the wayside where people gathered to listen to them. They would certainly draw a curious crowd, here were men from a foreign land bringing a revolutionary message to people who rarely left the immediate environs of their village. The first wooden crosses to be set up as permanent sites for preaching would be replaced with stone much later when Christianity was firmly established in a region.

In AD 634 when King Oswald of Northumbria was marching against the pagan king Penda of Mercia he found there was no church or altar at the place of battle called Heavenfield, seven miles north of Hexham, so he ordered a hole to be dug and a wooden cross set up. The king himself held the cross with both hands while the earth was thrown in, and ordered his army to kneel and pray for the safety of the nation. King Oswald's setting up of the cross before Heavenfield may have marked the beginning of the cult of the cross in Northumberland.

The cross was only adopted as an emblem of Christianity at the Council of Constantinople in AD 692. Prior to that date the fish was used as a Christian symbol. The use of the chi-rho cross traditionally dates from AD 312 when on the eve of the battle of Milvean Bridge, the emperor Constantine saw a vision of a cross in the sky accompanied by the words *'in hoc signo vinces'* (with this sign comes victory). Constantine gave orders for the symbol to be painted on his army's shields and after the victory he became a Christian and adopted the chi-rho as his emblem. The chi-rho takes its names from the letters of the Greek alphabet, chi (X) and rho (P) which are the initials of Jesus Christ in Greek.

Pope Gregory had instructed his missionaries not to indulge in the wholesale destruction of pagan shrines, but rather to convert the heathen temples to Christian use by replacing idols with altars. To convert the whole nation to Christianity was to take many years and there were times when pagan kings were able to overthrow the new religion and their followers revert to the old ways.

In AD 668 Theodore was consecrated archbishop by the Pope and set out for Britain that year reaching Canterbury in AD 669 and remained in office till his death in AD 690. The following extract is from Sir Frank Stenton's *'Anglo-Saxon England'*:

"Even at the end of the 8th century many Christian communities of long standing were still unprovided with any form of church. Archbishop Theodore had allowed priests to say mass 'in the field'. A century later, the life of St. Willibald, written by a nun of West Saxon origin, represents it as an English custom that on the estates of many lords there was no church, but only a cross raised on high for the daily service of prayer. The history of the standing cross in England is carried

Great Cross at Bewcastle, Cumbria

back to Theodore's time by a sentence in his book of canons enjoining that when a church has been removed to another place a cross should be erected on the site of the vanished altar.

Within a century of Theodore's arrival a succession of sculptors, working chiefly in Northumbria and northern Mercia, had produced a series of crosses decorated with sculpture of a quality unapproached elsewhere in Europe. Nothing definite is known about their teachers or the sources of their art, though there is reason to think that the vine scroll, which is the most distinctive of their many decorative motives, came to them from Italy. In any case, their fertility in designs and their mastery of the fantastic suggests that their work represents a sudden release of native artistic power which may have been assisted, but was never controlled, by motives supplied by foreign craftsmen. Naturally they were more successful in design, than in the representation of the human figure. Even so, the figure sculpture on their greatest works, the crosses of Bewcastle in Cumbria and Ruthwell in Dumfriesshire........is marked by almost classical poise and restraint."

Bewcastle is distant from the Peak, but is worth a visit if only to see the ancient cross with its splendid carvings. In addition to vine scrolls, human figures and interlaced knotwork, the south face bears a sundial.

The great number of coils given to the scrolls are a feature of several Derbyshire crosses and bear a close resemblance to work in Italy which reinforces the suggestion that the carvers were brought from that part of the world.

Also from Sir Frank Stenton's work we learn:

"Within 50 years of Ecgfrith's death (in AD 685), Whithorn, the most famous church of Galloway, had become the site of an English bishopric, and one of the greatest Northumbrian crosses had been erected at Ruthwell near Dumfries."

Most of our parish boundaries were set out by the Saxons in the years before the Norman Conquest and many of them still have the same ancient boundaries, or at least these boundaries can still be traced. This poses the question of whether crosses were set up as boundary markers or were already in position as way markers which could in many cases also be used to set out parish boundaries. Bearing the foregoing in mind I would suggest that the majority of the ancient crosses were erected from the eight century onwards and that the practice came to an end with the arrival of the Normans.

The Normans do not appear to have been very interested in crosses, preferring to build churches which seems eminently sensible, since nobody in their right mind would want to stand outside in the middle of winter in northern England listening to even the most inspiring preacher. When a new church was built on the site of a cross, the cross would become redundant. It might be moved and set up in the churchyard or used as building material for the church. Many of our older local parish churches have ancient carved stones preserved by building into the walls or set up in the porch.

The boundary between the Townships of Mellor and Thornsett is worthy of closer study. Starting at the northern end of the boundary is Robin Hood's Picking Rods, or the Maiden Stones as they were once known, the next marker heading south was the Stafforde Crosse which stood at approximately (SK004906). The next boundary marker was the site of the Old Pinfold followed by the Mislene (or Mishawe) and Briergreve Crosses at (SK002894) and (SJ997884) respectively along what we now know as Shiloh Road.

In his notes on the history of Glossop, written towards the end of the nineteenth century, Mr Robert Hamnett makes the following observations:

"A few years ago Mr Abner Frogatt found at the Ringstones a beautiful stone celt, or hand chisel and a peculiar stone hollowed out like the Abbot's Chair."

Robin Hood's Picking Rods

This could just be the base of the missing Mislene Cross.

At (SJ998881) if you peer over the wall at the junction of Shiloh Road and Moorend Road at a point formerly known as Jordanwall Nook, you will discover a large square stone half buried in the wall. Without demolishing the wall it is impossible to see if there is a mortice hole cut in the hidden face, but it certainly has the look of a cross base, and furthermore it is in the correct position for a wayside cross at a high point on the route from Mellor to Thornsett which also coincides with the junction of five roads. The boundary then follows Pole Lane as far as the site of Arnfield Pole at (SJ998877) before turning abruptly west-south-west along a field wall until it reaches Mellor Cross at the junction of Primrose Lane and Black Lane, (SJ993875). Thus there were formerly five, and probably seven crosses along a boundary of approximately two and a half miles. If this boundary was typical then it is reasonable to expect that there must have been dozens of crosses of which we now have no record. The manner in which the boundary changed direction at the Arnfield Pole is also worthy of note since an examination of old maps for similar changes might well indicate a site worthy of a closer look in the search for old crosses.

In '*Memorials of Old Derbyshire*' we read:

"*Arnfield Pole; This pole or cross is described in a survey of 1695 as parting the hamlets of Whittle, Thornset, and Mellor. At this spot, at the junction of two of the roads, there is a large piece of boulder stone, that has been roughly hewn, measuring 37ins by 25ins, and over the stone wall is another considerable fragment. These are probably the remains of the base of Arnfield Pole or Cross when it was broken up. Other crosses marked on the Mellor section of the 1640 map are respectively designated 'the Birgwurd Crosse', 'the Mislene Crosse', and the 'the Stafforde Crosse' "all of them on boundaries.*"

Mellor Cross

There is no sign of any large pieces of boulder sign today on the former site of Arnfield Pole but a little further south along the lane at (SJ997872) there are several large boulders and it appears that the Rev. Cox made a map reading error at this point.

The maps of 1640 are surprisingly accurate and therefore are a good guide to the position of crosses mentioned. Fig 1. shows representations of several of these crosses from the 1640 maps, but they are not all in the immediate Mellor/Thornsett area. They certainly seem to show that Arnfield Pole was once the site of a cross. In *Memorials of Old Derbyshire*, Rev. Cox states that the Birgwurd Cross was shown on the Mellor section of the 1640 map and also shows it as having two shafts. The site of the Birgwurd Cross is a subject I intend to return to later. On some of their maps, the surveyors refer to Mellor and Briergreve Crosses as Stone Crosses.

Before proceeding further it might be as well to point out that large stones embedded at the corners of drystone walls are fairly common in the Dark Peak and may have been

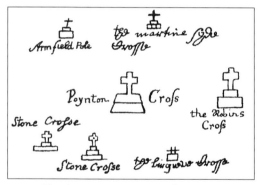

Fig 1: Representation of crosses on Map of 1640

placed there as a guide to the wall builders when the area was enclosed. Every one was not part of a cross base by any means. Large stones were also used to mark out the parish and township boundaries. A good example of one of these stones is at (SK023909) beside the track from Plainsteads Farm heading for Robin Hood's Picking Rods.

Writing in the *Athenaeum* of July 9th 1904 under the heading of '*Early Crosses in the High Peak*' the Rev. J Charles Cox refers to

Boundary Stone at SK022910 marking old
way to Ludworth

stone referred to by Rev. Cox. Mr Derek
Brumhead of the New Mills Local History
Society has suggested that as most of these
stones appear to be rounded they could well
be glacial stones removed from fields and
used as parish boundary markers long before
enclosure walls were built. The more of them
I see, the more I think he is correct.

In some instances crosses probably marked
the verge of a sanctuary. In medieval times
sanctuaries had a very important value in the
eyes of the law, both at home and abroad; and
Smollett, in his travels through France late in
the eighteenth century, mentions that:

*"All the churches are sanctuaries for all
kinds of criminals, except those guilty of
treason, and the priests are extremely
jealous of their privileges in this particular. They receive with open arms, murder-
ers, robbers, smugglers, fraudulent
bankrupts, and felons of every denomina-
tion, and never give them up, until after
having stipulated for their liberty.....I
saw a fellow who had three days before
murdered his wife in the last month of
pregnancy, taking the air with great com-
posure and serenity on the steps of a
church in Florence; and nothing is more
common than to see the most execrable
villains diverting themselves in the clois-
ters of some convents of Rome."*

this stone as being the rude base of a former
cross which had been later used as a direction
stone, the letters LUDW, for Ludworth, being
still legible. Another fragment of it is still in an
adjacent wall. From its present appearance
one would hesitate to pronounce this stone as
a cross base with any confidence, but there is
no doubt at all that it stands on a township
boundary between Simmondley and Thornsett
and alongside an old, once well-used track.
There is no trace of this lettering today nor
any other indication to confirm that this
rounded stone was once a cross base, but it is
certainly of a different appearance to the
stone used for local dry stone walls.

There is more to these large rounded stones
which can be found embedded into dry stone
walls, particularly where there is a change of
direction. Along the short straight stretch of
boundary between Chisworth and Thornsett
(SK012913-013911) there is a tumble-down
dry stone wall and at intervals along the
Chisworth side a few feet from the wall are
rounded boulders of the same material as the

In some of the older cathedrals and parish
churches, traces of the right of sanctuary are
still to be found. A fugitive criminal had the
right from Saxon times to take refuge in a
church or churchyard. After forty days there
he could confess before the Crown's repre-
sentative, abjure the realm and submit to
banishment rather than face trial. The Church
in medieval times was frequently in open
conflict with the authorities. A curious sanctuary door in Durham Cathedral is one example, and a more remarkable one is inside
Skipton parish church, where a large pillar,
supporting the transept, is hollowed out inside into a little sanctuary cell where the
hunted person could live, and escape seizure
by the officers of the law.

As social memorials, crosses were erected in commemoration of some great person. On Baslow Edge is a cross erected to commemorate Wellington, the victor at Waterloo. Edward I had twelve Queen Eleanor's crosses erected where her body rested each night during its last journey in 1290, thus we still have the names Charing and Waltham Cross. Of the twelve only three at Geddington, Hardingstone and Waltham Cross remain; the one outside Charing Cross Station is only a replica. If so many of the crosses erected by a king can disappear without trace we can only speculate on how many of the far older Saxon crosses once existed. More recently memorials to those who gave their lives in war have sometimes been in the form of a cross.

Market crosses stood at some popular rallying point where folks brought their produce. Sometimes they were hollowed out beneath into a polygonal vault with open sides, affording some shelter in bad weather for the folks attending the market. Local examples are at Bonsall on a base of 15 steps, Buxton, where only the stump remains, Chapel-en-le-Frith, Monyash, and Glossop.

In later years, the surviving shaft was frequently crowned with a sundial, as at Hope, and so, before the general advent of clocks, became a feature of the place, and according to Leyland, "a relic perhaps of the earliest times of Christianity in the Peak." Other familiar examples are Baslow, and Hathersage with sundial, 1811, by Daniel Rose, of Derwent.

Before examining local crosses there are a number of questions to be posed. When, where, and by whom were they carved? Various theories have been propounded to explain why there are different styles of crosses and as to who erected them and when. Crosses are variously described as Celtic, Saxon, and Runic and their design put down to the influence of Celtic monks from Ireland, or pagan symbols retained from the past by Saxons and Vikings. The widely differing standards of workmanship has been ascribed to cultures in

Wellington's Cross on Baslow Edge

Old Glossop Market Cross

decline for no very obvious reason.

There are certainly styles of crosses which tend to be grouped in certain areas. The Mercian round-shafted crosses for example are to be found in Cheshire, Staffordshire and north-west Derbyshire, an area which coincides with the land of a tribe known as the Pecsaetna. Rectangular shafted crosses carved with ornate interlaced patterns and depictions of scenes from the Bible are to be found at Eyam, Bakewell, Sheffield, Hope and Bradbourne in an area which generally lies on the East side of the Pennines. It is impossible to say that one type of cross is exclusive to an area. In Leek churchyard there is a round shafted cross and a rectangular sculpted one nearby. What we do not know is how long they have been there and where they stood originally.

When I was at school a simplified version of history was taught in which blond blue-eyed Celts drove out the original inhabitants, only to be driven westward in turn by Germanic tribes, followed by blond blue-eyed Vikings,

followed yet again by the Normans who as descendants of Vikings would be blond and blue-eyed. One could be excused for wondering why the entire population of England does not consist of blond blue-eyed people. Clearly the true situation was much more complex with conquerors taking over the best of the land and the former owners being forced onto poorer upland areas.

There would surely be intermarriage and numbers of the original inhabitants still tilling the soil under the overlordship of the new owners. If Celtic or formerly pagan Saxon masons were employed to carve a piece of stone it should come as no surprise if they incorporated a few ideas of their own. Anyone who has had any dealings with tradesmen knows that the hardest thing to do is to get them to do the task in the way you want it. Despite the fact that you are the one paying for the work, if you turn your back for an instant they will introduce a few innovations of their own which may or may not be improvements.

Cross in Baslow Churchyard

Bonsal Market Cross

This also brings into question how many men were employed in carving crosses. Several crosses have so many features in common that it suggests they are the work of the same man or at least of a small group. It would take a mason several months to carve a complete cross, but this does not pose a problem, speed was not the important thing, after all it took centuries to build a cathedral with sons following fathers at the work. In later centuries the master masons who built the cathedrals moved across Europe from Hungary to England taking their ideas and skills with them, so it would be no great step for a mason who had carved a cross in Bernicia to move on to Derbyshire if his services were in demand there.

The suggestion that the standard of sculpture declined because the local culture was also in decline seems suspect to me. I can suggest several alternative explanations which would be obvious to anyone who has tried their hand at constructive work. The quality of stone available varies considerably; millstone grit in some beds can be extremely coarse with embedded quartz pebbles while in others it is a smooth even sandstone. A few years ago a small stone cross was excavated in the grounds of Carlisle cathedral. Due to its long sojourn in the soil, the cross was exceedingly well preserved as was a cold chisel found with it. It would be interesting to learn how this chisel was made. This is a topic which seems to have been conveniently ignored. If you think it a simple matter to cut stone, then I suggest that you get hold of a cold chisel and try your hand on a piece of granite.

This calls into question the quality of the tools available to these medieval workmen. Without chisels capable of cutting the hardest rocks, the masons would have no choice but to opt for the best material they could work with. Fortunately it is easier to work sandstones when they are in the "green" state, straight out of the quarry before the stone has dried out and hardened.

As to where they were made, it is reasonable to assume that they were carved close to the source of the stone and moved to their destination on a sledge or cart drawn by oxen.

An examination of Eyam, Bakewell and Bradbourne crosses shows that they have much in common in the style of carving. This is not to say that they are all the work of one man, but masons certainly have styles of workmanship. There must have been plenty of masons who could cut stone accurately to size and give it the desired finish, but the carving of crosses and gargoyles calls for a degree of artistry as well. Presumably those who showed an aptitude for such work would have been in demand and expect to be adequately paid for their skills.

The designs actually carved into the stone are the reason why we read of crosses being Celtic, Saxon or Runic. The problem is that we do not really know how men in the eight century thought. A winged figure blowing a trumpet might be recognised by us as a depiction of an angel, but what of all the whorled shapes? Are they intended to show winding foliage added merely as ornamentation, or are they some representation of pagan beliefs? One could imagine some of them as snakes with the tails of other snakes in their mouths. Several crosses have the figure of an archer carved near the base of the shaft. He is shooting an arrow at some small animal hiding among the foliage higher up. Does this convey some religious message? Or is it the sculptor expressing his individuality?

One design which appears on the arms of many crosses is the triquetra with its three interlaced arcs. This can be explained as representing the trinity, but there are similar shapes with four arcs to be found at the centre of cross heads. The explanation might be much simpler; the triquetra fits in very well with the shape of the cross arm.

If you look at a painting executed by an Australian aboriginal artist it is usually easy to pick out a snake or turtle or some other creature, but only someone who understands aboriginal culture can explain the story that is being depicted. In a similar manner the medieval mason was telling a story in stone which we cannot always comprehend. Another factor which makes the carvings harder to understand is that some crosses have been exposed to the elements for over a thousand years and we can only surmise on their appearance when new.

Before going on to look a various crosses in some detail it is as well to bear in mind the various reasons that have been put forward for the siting of crosses. These vary from preaching crosses where folks could gather to listen to itinerant preachers; way markers set up to guide travellers in districts where there were no proper roads; way markers leading to churches set up when they were few and far between; boundary markers for parishes or monastery lands; to crosses which once stood on the site before a church was built. Hopefully it should be possible to come to some definite conclusions before we have finished our journey.

2 BOUNDARY CROSSES

The crosses of the area have been divided into convenient groups as far as is possible. This is a far from easy task as several could be listed under more than one heading; a cross standing beside an ancient track can also be a boundary marker, or for that matter a preaching cross. Over the centuries crosses have been moved for reasons varying from the whim of councillors, to a desire to hide them from those intent on destruction. Some crosses now standing in churchyards are former market or wayside crosses moved to their present sites for safe keeping, their original positions often being a matter for conjecture. Yet another difficulty is that with the discovery of each cross site, fresh questions are posed as to the reasons why it was placed there.

To imagine what the English countryside was like during the centuries before the crosses were erected we would need to blot out most of the fields, hedges and walls, and all the modern roads which we take for granted. There would be none of the signposts or tall buildings to act as landmarks and over rough moorland and in thinly inhabited areas it would be easy to lose the right track. In such a wilderness a tall cross mounted at the summit of a pass or at intervals along the track would have been invaluable, even to those who knew the route. The constant passage of travellers would eventually cut a furrow across the land and we come across these, at first, seemingly pointless, ruts on moorlands to this day.

Parish boundaries were delineated in a number of ways; by streams and rivers; by existing roads; by field fences, and by prominent natural features such as long lived oaks and thorns. The custom of beating the bounds was once found in every English parish and usually involved walking around or to the parish boundary and beating the various mark points with a stick, or stripped willow branch known as a wand. On occasion the boys were beaten as well as the mark stones to ensure that they remembered where the marks were. The practice is probably of Pagan origin and there may be some significance in the use of willow wands as the willow was a sacred tree of the druids. Whatever its origins it was certainly taken over by the church. In 470 AD there was a serious earthquake in plague ridden Vienne, in France, and the bishop ordered litanies to be said in solemn procession through the fields on Ascension Day. In 511 AD this custom was extended to the whole of Gaul and by the early eighth century had been officially adopted in England.

The ceremony was once regarded as important. There were several reasons for walking the bounds. One was to learn where the boundaries lay in the days before there were reliable maps. Another was to check that none of the marker stones had been moved in an effort to claim one's land. It also provided an opportunity for the priest to bless the field and crops. Beating the bounds took place on Rogation Days when solemn supplications consisting of the litany of the saints were chanted during procession on the three days before Ascension Day. Hence Rogation Sunday is the 5th Sunday after Easter, being the Sunday before Ascension Day. The ceremony was a great opportunity for poor folks to have a celebration and it had the added advantage of bringing the community together. Garlands made from the cross-flower, or rogation flower, or gang flower were carried in the procession. We know it as the common milkwort today.

The trouble with written history is that it is mainly concerned with the doings of the high and mighty and we only rarely get a glimpse of what ordinary folks thought about the upheavals in religion. I would imagine that most would have enjoyed a good procession with a distribution of cakes and ale and a couple of days off work as a bonus. The great destruction of books during the reformation by both parties is one of the reasons we have difficulty in finding details of these processions and other observances. Sometimes we get a glimpse of the past such as an entry in the Churchwarden's accounts for Hope in 1688-89 where there is an entry, *"Spent in going with the perambulation 4s 6d."* Many of these old customs were swept away or became only a shadow of their former importance. Indeed they were condemned by some

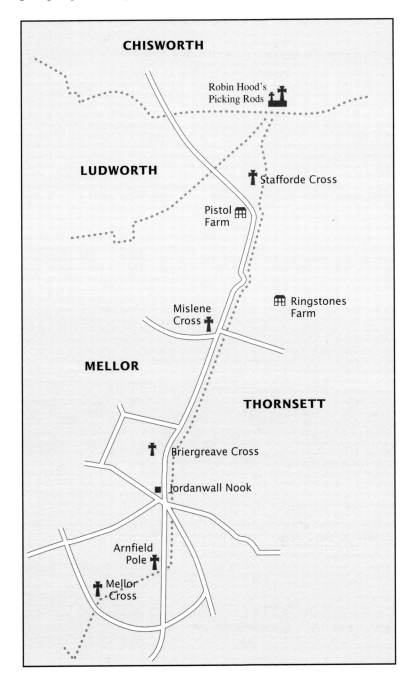

Map 1: Mellor/Thornsett Boundary

who held that the observation of Gangdays, or Rogation Days was wholly Popish.

During the reigns of Elizabeth I and Charles II Royal Charters were issued laying down that this ancient historical custom be carried out annually during the days of Rogation, that the minister shall at convenient places admonish the people to give thanks to God for the increase and abundance of the fruits of the earth with the saying of Psalm 104. The minister shall also inculcate this sentence: "Cursed be he which translateth the bounds and doles of his neighbours."

Various minor officials were required in beating the bounds; the Axeman to clear obstacles along the boundary; the Banner Bearer; and where the boundary followed a river, the Wader to carry the minister into the middle to read out his proclamation. In some parishes it was the custom to carry in the procession a standard of a dragon with a long tail representing the Devil, and on the last day when the congregation marched back to the church the standard had lost its tail to show that the Devil had been driven from the parish. This could lead to some interesting situations when members of two parishes met at the boundary on the last day and were not pleased to think that the Devil was being driven into their parish. Building a house astride the boundary could also be a hazardous business as the owner might find the whole procession trooping through on Rogation day.

I make no claim to telling the age of crosses accurately but can certainly give a few pointers as to where to find them. As a general rule the older six inch maps are the most useful as there is a tendency for later maps to have excluded them after the remains have disappeared either by removal or under bricks and mortar. The fact that there is no indication of a cross on the map does not mean that there were none in the area. The places to look are along routes which were once old trackways and sometimes coincide with a parish boundary. Crosses alongside old ways are usually placed at a high point where they would act as a guide to travellers. This positioning was done so carefully that it is often possible to know fairly accurately where they stood even when not a stone remains on the spot. Martinside and Charlesworth crosses are typical examples. Always be suspicious of large stones which are obviously different to stones in nearby walls as this implies that they have been brought from a distance.

Abbot's Chair

(SK029903) Looks exactly like the broken base of a substantial cross, which it undoubtedly is. It has a small circular depression in its top face like some market crosses. The

The Abbot's Chair near Monks Road

name like Monk's Road, probably comes from the Abbots of Basingwerk who held the land in the Middle Ages. The Abbot's Chair has been known by that name since at least 1640 when it appeared on a map. The odd thing about the Abbot's Chair is that it is some distance from the modern Monk's Road, but is on the line of the much older Roman Road from Edrotalia to Buxton. In fact the Roman Road made a turn at this point; probably just another example of a modern road following the general line of a Roman Road but offset somewhat to one side or the other when the older road became impassable. The township boundary between Chunal and Hayfield makes a right angled turn at the Abbot's Chair and heads for the Hollingworth Head Cross on the opposite side of Monks Road. The shaft which once stood in this base must have been of a considerable size and one can only wonder where it went.

In the sixteenth century most folks still lived in wooden cruck style houses, or wattle and daub shacks, but it was from about this time that the first substantial stone built farmhouses began to be appear. An overthrown cross shaft would be the very thing to use as a lintel, especially when it seemed that it was no longer required. In the fullness of time some might yet appear when old farms and barns are demolished or renovated.

Ball Cross

Ball Cross. The base of Ball Cross has disappeared but it stood beside the packhorse way from Bakewell to Sheffield and Chesterfield. Ballcross Farm is at (SK227695). Burdett's map shows the site of the Ballcross at a road fork at (SK235698) and there is a guide stoop still in existence here. The most promising site for the Ball Cross is at a kink in the boundary between the civil parishes of Bakewell and Edensor at (SK228694) just to the east of Ballcross Farm. This site also coincides with a high point along the track. On the Victorian Ordnance Survey map, the name of the farm is spelled Bow Cross which may very well reflect the mapmakers translation

of the local Derbyshire dialect. I can recall playing 'footbow' in Whitfield schoolyard as a boy.

In the Derbyshire Countryside for October, 1940, appears an article by Mr. R.W.P. Cockerton entitled, "Ancient Roads at Bakewell.' In it he makes reference to writing by Mr. John Taylor who was a great-great uncle of Mr. Cockerton.

"I found yesterday, 19th October, 1820, the Pedestal of the old Cross which stood on Ball Cross above Bakewell. It is well placed on the very brow of the hill, so as to be seen from below as well as from a distance; the stone is about 32 inches diameter square, with a circular socket in the middle for the shaft which formed the pillar; this hole is about 16 inches diameter and 7 inches deep. From a comparison of other pillars (the one at Middleton) with the dimensions of this as given by the width of the socket, it would seem to have been according to the same proportions at least 10 feet high. This pillar probably was broken to pieces to mend the road with, as Mr. Gauntley, Agent to the Duke of Rutland, some years ago ordered a Column standing in the road above the Butts leading to Youlgreave to (be) destroyed for that purpose, and the base of it at this time forms a cheese press in Mr. G. Heathcote's house. The road up to Ball Cross was formerly paved throughout, but Mr. Holmes and another person had the major part of these stones broken up to mend the road; he says the road does not extend its pavement beyond the top of the hill and that 60 years ago, when he came daily down it to go to school it was almost as deeply worn as any parts of it are now.

The old road on leaving Bakewell appears to have gone over Ball Cross. Traces of a paved way are discernible by the side of the castle Hill round which it partially wound. Since writing this I have been informed by Mr G. Holmes that there is the remnant of another Cross on Ball

Part of Thomas Bateman's Collection in
Bakewell Church

*Cross – another in a field beyond the Croft
House, on the left of of the present road,
and another on the hill over the Butts
towards Alport, called Stump Cross."*

This reference is intriguing; to describe the
base as 32ins diameter square is somewhat
confusing; but the socket is definitely described as circular which suggests a large
Mercian pillar type cross. If this is so, then it
is the most easterly example known. A column standing in the road leading to
Youlgreave also suggests a pillar cross.

The Middleton by Youlgrave cross was
carried away by Thomas Bateman to
Lomberdale Hall and presumably is now

among the remnants restored to Bakewell
church in 1899 by Weston Park Museum,
among which are both round and rectangular
cross sections.

Mr Cockerton's account gives details of
two further crosses near Bakewell. One of
these was situated near Croft House between
Bakewell and Ball Cross which, if to the left of
the present road, would be at approximately
SK224691 some distance from where the old
packhorse way climbed the hill. The other
opposite Shutts Farm, stood beside the
Bakewell-Conksbury Bridge-Youlgrave road
about half a mile SSW of the cross in Butts
Road. The most likely site is at SK212672
where the ancient Portway branches off Yeld
Road, because on the 1799 map from the
Manor of Haddon there is a field named as
Stump Cross close by. Another possible site is
at SK212678 where Shutts Lane meets Yeld
Road. So along the route of the old way from
Youlgrave to Bakewell and on to Sheffield
and Chesterfield we have at least three
crosses. (Map 2).

The Birley Stone

An Ecclesfield carpenter, Septimus Lister left
a diary and among the entries for 1792/3 is
the following:

Birley Stone

"William Lister of Birley Edge, Died January 2nd. (Birley Edge is in so bleak a situation that a local wit said that he did not shave on a Sunday morning, but just went up to the base of the cross there and stuck first one side and then the other side of his face out, and the wind shore off his whiskers as clean as a whistle.)"

Birley Edge is built up today, but at (SK325934) is the Birley Stone standing at a zig-zag on the Ecclesfield boundary and also

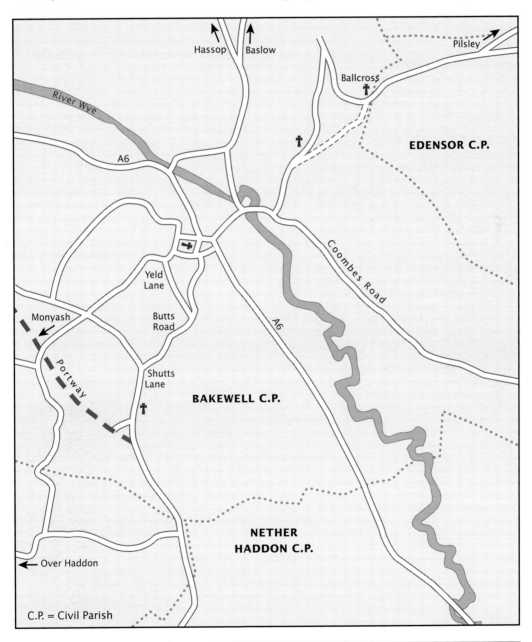

Map 2: Crosses in the Bakewell Area

beside the road between Ecclesfield church and Bradfield church.

The Birley Stone consists of a large base 45 inches by 34 inches and 18 inches high with a column with a rounded top 19 by 11 inches and 53 inches high set upright in it. If this is not the remains of the Birley Cross, then we have another cross in the area.

Catshaw Cross

Remains of the shaft of Catshaw Cross

(SE205035) This stood beside the old road from Penistone to Holmfirth. All that can be seen today is a vertical stone set in the wall which is probably the remains of the shaft. The dry stone wall surrounding this stone has been rebuilt recently and it is a matter for congratulation that the craftsman who did the job saw fit to leave the stone in situ rather than using it as walling material. It is situated slightly to the west of a rise in the road on the north side. It would be the ideal site for a wayside cross and way marker being visible to anyone approaching from either direction.

Charlesworth Cross

(SK019924), is not marked on modern maps but the site was indicated on the 1899 6ins map. It was located at the summit of Monks Road where it would act as a guidepost to travellers approaching from either direction, standing beside one of the earliest ways to cross the southern Pennines continuing eastwards past the Abbot's Chair to Edale Cross. It also marked the boundary between the townships of Simmondley and Charlesworth. Where are the remains? Well the site is ideal for the type of person who likes rolling stones downhill and a careful search of the steep hillside below might reveal broken fragments.

Charlesworth Cross was situated at a fine vantage point with splendid views across Lancashire and Cheshire to the west; Mouselow and Longdendale to the north; Shire Hill, Bleaklow and the entrance to Doctor's Gate to the north east; and finally the route of the Roman Road up Bray Clough.

Crossgate Farm

(SK140761) Along the road once known as Kirkgate (the gate leading to the church), or Crossgate heading west out of Tideswell there is a cross base near Crossgate Farm. I had an interesting conversation with the farmer who told me that his family had been there since the 1800s, but he was not aware of any cross shafts about the property. He did however point out the "wishing well" a little further along the road. This turned out to be the weathered base of a cross which coincided with the boundary between Wheston and Tideswell Civil Parishes. He also told of an attempted theft of the base some years ago. Stone water troughs and carved stones of various sorts have become collectors items and can command high prices which could lead to the disappearance of more antiquities. This cross is one of the few shown on the Victorian Ordnance Survey map.

Crossgate Nr Tideswell. Known locally as a 'Wishing Well'.

Eccles Pike Cross.

Now for a spot of detective work. The following description of the discovery of a cross shaft buried in a wall comes from the *Victoria History of Derbyshire* and shows how an observant person knowing where to look can find an ancient artifact:

"A cross shaft 4 feet 8 inches high and 1 foot 3 inches wide at the broadest part, tapering to 12 inches was discovered in 1903 by Mr WJ Andrew in a rough stone boundary wall on Eccles Pike, in the parish of Chapel-en-le-Frith. It was almost entirely hidden by the masonry of the wall, but when this was taken away it was seen to be set in a rough stone base 2 feet 10 inches in diameter and 10 inches high above ground level, and it appeared that the cross was in situ, there being no evidence of its ever having been out of its socket. The shaft is complete, the head only of the cross having been lost, and

both faces and sides are covered with interlaced patterns within cable borders."

Writing in the *Athenaeum* in July 1904, the Rev J. Charles Cox says:

"Mr Andrew found a tall Saxon cross shaft, well worked on each side, in the midst of one of the high field walls of north Derbyshire, not far from his residence at Cadster House, between Chapel-en-le-Frith and Whaley Bridge. Its exact position cannot be given for fear of trespass, and after being carefully photographed it has been built up again into the wall. This too, is at an angle of an old boundary line."

Eccles Pike Cross. Now in the churchyard of St Thomas Becket, Chapel en le Frith.

The following year writing once more in the *Athenaeum* Rev. Cox describes this cross shaft as follows:

> "The wall up each side of it giving the appearance of a disused stone gatepost. It may be added that the hill on the side of which the cross stands is called Eccles Pike, a suggestive name. The cross is certainly of the Derbyshire churchyard type, and has no resemblance to pillar stones, such as the Picking Rods."

If the cross was still in situ in the field wall then it would be a simple matter to find it from Rev. Cox's articles. Ollerenshaw Hall Farm stands on Eccles Pike and there are three angles in the boundary between Chapel-en-le-Frith and Whaley Bridge within a stones throw of the farm, all being likely contenders for the site of the cross. The road passing the farm is an old saltway which should make (SK025807) the most likely.

However, a search is unnecessary because around 1925 a cross was moved from Ollerenshaw Farm to Chapel-en-le-Frith churchyard for safe keeping and stood near the north-west corner of the church tower where it marked the grave of the farmer, a Mr Hodgson. In 1973 it became necessary to move the cross again to make way for the building of the extension to the church known as the Becket Room. The move was carried out by Mr Arthur Hibbert and his son Peter who was 12 at the time.

I have no doubt that the cross in Chapel Churchyard and the cross found on Eccles Pike are one and the same as the dimensions are identical. The cross shaft is very worn but the outlines of plaits and whorls similar to Hope and other crosses can be made out which matches the description of the Eccles Pike Cross given by Rev. Cox. It also is mounted in what appears to be an old round base which also agrees with Mr Andrew's account.

It seems entirely appropriate that the ancient cross from Ollerenshaw Farm should have been placed in Chapel-en-le-Frith churchyard standing over the farmer's

remains. Plenty of farmers have a copse or a pond on their property, but how many have a Roman Road, an ancient burial ground, or other site of historical interest about the place. I would imagine they would take a certain pride in such a possession. I knew a farmer who had a Roman Road running within yards of his front door. He made it his business to keep the road in order as the kerbstones tended to move down the slope towards the river.

At this point it might be as well to ask why should some crosses have a plain rectangular shaft while others are carved with ornate designs? It might be expected that the so called High Crosses with carvings of religious scenes and complicated scrolls and knotwork would be found at, or close to, early churches such as Bakewell or Hope. This might apply in a few cases but Beeley and Eccles Pike Crosses have carved shafts and used to stand beside moorland tracks, and several which now stand in churchyards are reputed to have been brought there from outer parts of the parish for safe keeping.

Edale Cross

(SK077861) Stands under Kinder Low, once again sited at the summit of a bridle road, this time the one from Hayfield to Edale at an altitude of around 1750 feet. Although rather crude in execution, this cross does not look particularly old and may not be the first to stand on what is undoubtedly an ancient site being the junction of the three wards of the Forest of Peak; that is Glossop and Longdendale; Hopedale, and the Campagna or open southern portion. The original cross may have been set up in the first place by the Cistercian Abbots of Basingwerk Abbey at the southern boundary of land included in the grant of the manor and parish of Glossop which they received from Henry II in 1157.

The Rev. Dr. Cox was of the opinion that the marking on the head was IG 1610 and alluded to a boundary survey of parts of the Forest begun in that year which was never completed, the initials referring to John Gell,

THIS MEDIAEVAL CROSS
IS PROTECTED AS A
MONUMENT OF NATIONAL
IMPORTANCE UNDER THE
NCIENT MONUMENTS ACTS
1913-53
MINISTRY OF PUBLIC BUILDING & WORKS

Edale Cross at the Summit of the packhorse way between Hayfield and Edale

the commissioner, who was probably a member of the Gell family who lived at the Parsonage House at Bakewell; now the Old House Museum.

On this occasion Rev. Cox was wide of the mark. The date is 1810 and years before this the old cross was thrown down and lay embedded in the peat for ages. The cross was re-erected by Mr John Gee of the Ashes, Kinder, and four of his farmer friends in 1810, hence the date. The small initials WD, GH, JH, and JS on the cross refer to William Drinkwater who was probably from the now deserted ruin of Hollin Head Farm; George and Joseph Hadfield of Upper Booth and John Shirt of The Lee Farm, Edale. Mr Gee cut his initials into it along with the year 1810 with the sharp point of a pick. Formerly it was taller but a large portion of the shaft has been broken off, probably when it was thrown down. No trace of the base remains. Formerly the cross stood behind the wall, the supporting wall not being built until about the year 1838.

Edale Cross is rather coarsely finished, but this may due to the nature of the millstone grit at the site rather than a reflection on the skill of the mason. On the sides of this cross appear the letters H and M which could well denote the ancient parishes of Hopedale and Middlecale.

Fulshaw Cross

The cross roads at (SE211016) are commonly referred to as Fulshaw Cross. A packhorse way and later the first turnpike road from Manchester passed by this point and carried on past Hartcliffe Farm en route to Rotherham. I note that the parish boundary between Penistone and Stocksbridge passes along the A628 here and that the boundary between Penistone and Dunford makes a right angle with this road at SE206016 and then heads almost due north to Catshaw Cross. Because there is a crossroads at Fulshaw Cross this is not a good enough reason for assuming that the cross stood there. The new turnpike road was not made until 1830 and there may not even have been a track down to

Millhouse before that date. We shall return to Fulshaw Cross in connection with other crosses along the route to Penistone (p.36).

Great Hucklow

G.H.B. Ward mentions the base of a cross, with mortise, at the roadside, near the Queen Anne Inn and makes the suggestion that it was the remains of the local Poynton Cross. I have failed to find any trace of this cross base in Great Hucklow, but at (SK160777) stands Poyntoncross Barn beside the road from Tideswell to Little Hucklow at the junction of the civil parishes of Great and Little Hucklow and Tideswell, which would have been a likely site for the Poynton Cross. There is also a Poyntoncross House a quarter of a mile to the east and quite close to the parish boundary.

Harrop Edge Cross

Harrop Edge Cross Base

(SJ981957) A rather large and crudely worked cross base on the boundary between Mottram and Matley, standing close to the junction in the tracks opposite Cheetham Fold Farm. The base has several holes cut into its upper surface like those cut into some market crosses. This base could also stand on the line of the same Roman Road as Ashtonhill Cross, but the construction of by-passes and the motorway has altered the whole appearance of the area.

Hollingworth Head Cross

Hollingworth Head Cross Base situated on opposite side of Monks Road to the Abbot's Chair.

(SK030904) Only the base remains standing in a field just off Monks Road, the shaft is believed to be buried in a wall nearby. This base is quite obvious to anyone looking over the wall as it is close to the road, but few seem to know of its whereabouts. It is much smaller than the one on the opposite side of Monks Road known as the Abbot's Chair. Both are boundary markers, the boundary between the Townships of Chunal and Hayfield making sudden diversions to accommodate them. This base has the letters N and R plus a cross cut into it. Why is it known as Hollingworth cross? The only explanation I can offer is that the nearby farm is called Hollingworth Head Farm, (known locally as Hollieth Head), and there is a Hollingworth Clough running from Mill Hill not all that far away. Many Pennine farms take their names from former tenants and Hollingworth is a local surname although I have failed to

find a trace of anyone of that name living in the immediate neighbourhood in the past.

Robert Hamnett writes that Mr J.D. Doyle found a portion of the head of the cross in a wall nearby, and suggests that he would be willing to give it to the Glossop Museum. If Mr Doyle did donate the piece of cross head as suggested, it could well have been transferred to Buxton Museum with the other antiquities.

The south-east end of Monks Road provides an excellent example of how a stretch of ancient way can disappear and leave no trace on the ground. From the site of Hollingworth Head Cross the old way kept straight on to meet the A624 at (SK033903). It then went on following a still obvious route on the opposite side of the main road to cross Hollingworth Clough and eventually pass by Edale Cross. Several sections of this route had been cut deep into the earth to form distinct hollow ways. The section from Hollingworth Head Cross to the A624 passed out of use with the construction of the present Monks Road and it soon became a tip for old cars and other junk. The farmer removed this eyesore by filling in the hollow and grassing it over to make a useful small field. The old way was the only one shown on Burdett's map; both routes were marked on the Victorian Ordnance map, but by 1895 it was no longer worthy of mention.

Hollins Cross

(SK136846) Stood at a high point on the ridge way and path from Edale to Castleton, which was once known as the coffin road as laden coffins were carried this way from Edale to the Hope church before Edale church was built. Nothing remains but it is still marked on modern maps. The Rev. J Charles Cox could find no trace of Hollins Cross in 1905.

Lady Cross

Lady Cross at the Summit of the Woodhead Pass.

(SK148998) For some reason this is one of the best known crosses in the region and is shown on maps of various vintages, despite being located on a track used only by hikers. Stands at the summit of the old packhorse and early turnpike road from Longdendale to Rotherham. It marks the limit of the lands of the Abbots of Basingwerk, and also served as a boundary marker between the Townships of Thurlstone and Langsett. The stump of the shaft is badly damaged but it would be a typical wayside cross in its heyday, and is still clearly visible to travellers approaching from either direction.

The tapering base of the cross is 3ft by 2ft 8ins and the top 2ft 4ins. The mortice hole is about 11 inches square. The letters IWB; WB; and MB, have been rudely carved into the sides of the base, but these marks are relatively modern and have nothing to do with surveying.

Lady's Cross

(SK272782) A wayside cross on Big Moor, which stood beside the way from Froggat to Chesterfield, it was first mentioned in a document of 1263 and is said to have served as a marker for the junction of the boundaries of Hathersage, Holmesfield and Totley, although this junction lies some distance to the south-west. This is an excellent example of the difficulty of placing crosses in a definite category. Only a short section of the shaft remains set in a square base. The 'Sheffield Clarion Ramblers Journal' contains a photograph of this cross with the broken off part of the shaft set up roughly in position and contains the following information:

> "Lady's Cross is 300 yards west of Barbrook Bridge and stands almost at the summit of the moor. You would run all the risks and penalties of trespass if you went to see it. Yet it should be a national monument and be well protected and railed off, for anyone to see and to learn from it; because it gives good history and education to any tramp.
>
> Lady's Cross goes back 660 years. (In the opinion of G.H.B. Ward). It lies beside the deep-trenched, forgotten bridle-ways which led from Hope and Hathersage to Chesterfield (by Hollowgate, and across Longshaw Park) and from Tideswell to Dronfield, long before coach and carriage roads in this part of Derbyshire were dreamed of. Some day we will describe it and see how our fathers pursued the way on packhorse in the days of the merry Catholic kings.
>
> The present cross is the modern one of Puritan days. They had a mania for destroying old wayside shrines and crosses where the wanderer could say one or two sacred words and cross himself on his weary upland way between market, church, and home. Today the base of the cross is a stone 2ft 1ins x 1ft 6ins, having a square hole in the centre to hold the base of a rectangular shaft, 4ft 6ins in height and 12ins x 12ins. The shaft has

Lady's Cross on Big Moor.

been broken and taken out in order not to draw the curious to it from the main road."

Here we have another reason for the destruction of crosses; all the blame cannot be laid on Oliver Cromwell's soldiery by any means. Its existence would confirm that it had once been a public right of way:

"On the south east side of the cross base are two small chiselled crosses as ++. On the north east side are the letters I.R. 1618; possibly the initials of the then lord of the Manor of Hathersage, the cross lying at the boundary thereof; and on the front of the north east side is a letter T. It is likely that the monks of Beauchief Abbey put the Lady's Cross as a landmark of their western boundary of the free grazing lands."

In an article on the 'Saltways From The Cheshire Wiches,' W.B. Crump shows a salt route from Grindleford Bridge to Dronfield passing by the Lady's Cross which suggests there was a way marker there long before there was an Abbey at Beauchief.

Mellor Cross

The heavy square base of Mellor Cross stands set in the wall at the junction of Primrose Lane and Black Lane, at (SJ993875). It lies on the boundary between Mellor and New Mills at an angle on Mellor Moor (enclosed in 1676). According to the Rev. Cox there stood a cross, apparently perfect, at this point in the seventeeth century. Almost a mile to the west of Mellor Cross at (SJ978872) is a property called Cross Gates which lies along a track leading to Black Lane and the cross. This base has been turned into a signpost by the expedient of placing a stout square wooden shaft into the base.

Moscar Cross

Today the name Moscar Cross refers to a guide stoop which was set up to comply with an Act of Parliament of 1702 and stands at (SK231883) along a parish boundary and at the junction of two old packhorses tracks.

It bears the inscriptions:-

SHEF	BRAD	HATHER	HOPE
FEILD	FIELD	SAGE	ROA(D)
		ROAD	

respectively on its faces.

It is always possible that an existing cross shaft was dressed and converted into a guide post but not in this instance, I think.

There was certainly a cross nearby long before guide stoops were set up. In '*A boundary*

Moscar Cross an 18th century Guide Stoop

of *Hathersage Manor,*' sworn by jury on 28.8.1571, it is called Humblestone Cross, and in an '*ancient bounds and limits of the manor of Hathersage,*' sworn on 7.8.1656 "Hamblestone Cross, alias Moscar Cross."

The remnant of a base was found in the field called Parson's Piece by Terry Howard, and the cross was standing 50 metres north of the guide stoop on Moscar Cross Lane in the eighteenth century.

If you travel east along the old track which passes close to Moscar farm until you come to a stile at approximately (SK233884) you will find that the stones forming the stile consist of large rectangular blocks and at the opposite end of the gate lie three stones. Two of these are tapered and might once have formed a cross shaft while the third is reminiscent of the head of Whibbersley Cross. These stones are crudely shaped and Humblestone might serve as a good description. They are worthy of a closer examination as they did not get to their present position on their own. One possible explanation is that they once stood upright and acted as a way marker.

Oxlow Cross

This cross stood once not far from the top of the Winnats Pass beside the turnpike road, and there is an Oxlow House at (SK125825) at the roadside and lying on the parish boundary between Castleton and Chapel-en-le-Frith. I have examined the walls at each side of the road close to Oxlow House, but have failed to find any trace of a cross shaft or base.

Crosses to the West of Penistone

Near the junction of Cross Lane and Hartcliffe Road; (SE235021), sited in a field at some distance from the road, but clearly visible, is a cross shaft and base, said by some to have been the Penisale Market Cross erected by Richard Lovetot (c1134), but by others to have been only a guide for travellers over what was formerly part of the open moor. The second explanation seems the more likely. This cross stands between Midhope and Penistone Church. In the days when Penistone Church was the nearest place of worship for Midhope folks, this cross would stand on open moorland.

Part of Hartcliffe Road was a packhorse route into Penistone before the making of the turnpike road and with the enclosure of land, the route would be diverted and the cross left isolated at some distance from the present road.

The base is rectangular 32 x 37ins and 20ins in height. The corners are chamfered off in a similar manner to the Lady Cross and the cross standing in Penistone churchyard. The shaft is rectangular tapering from 14 x 11ins at the bottom to 12 x 9ins at the top. The corners have been chamfered off from about 10ins above the base. An indistinct letter T can be seen on the west face of the shaft and near the bottom of the south face the smaller letters HA.

This cross is not situated on any boundary today, but during the research into the origins and reasons for its siting, some fascinating facts have emerged which give a much more likely explanation of the origins of this cross. A map was unearthed by Mr Barry Shaw, which must have been drawn around the year 1800. The map takes the form of a sketch produced by the Sheffield architects Fairbank apparently in connection with some dispute over the boundary of Langsett and neighbouring parishes. The map was drawn with a quill pen as evidenced by the many ink splashes, but many places and features known today can be picked out. The main interest is that it indicates the existence of four and possibly five additional crosses.

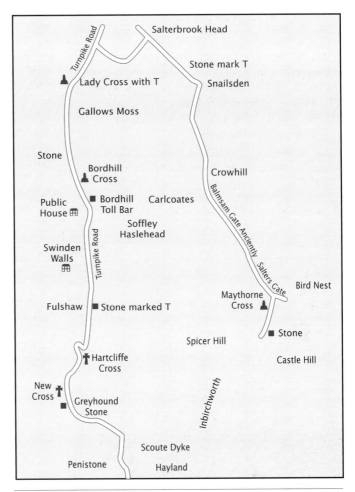

Map 3: Crosses Along Penistone to Saltersbrook Turnpike

Starting from Penistone the road appears to have climbed Hornthwaite Hill and headed for the Greyhound Stone. The first cross shown is marked as the New Cross, located to the west of the Greyhound Stone which today marks a sudden departure of the boundary away from Hartcliffe Road. At first this seems odd because if the New Cross is the same as the one now at (SE235021) then it has been moved from its original site. This is a distinct possibility as local tradition says the cross was once closer to the road, and if it was west of the Greyhound Stone it would have stood on the parish boundary. If it has not been moved then there is another cross site waiting to be discovered, unless of course Messrs Fairbank omitted it from their drawing.

The Greyhound Stone is a well known local boundary marker mentioned in the survey of Langsett and Thurlstone in 1695. It was also mentioned in the Rogation Day perambulations of of the sixteenth, seventeenth and eighteenth

New Cross near junction of Cross Lane and Hartcliffe Road. (Provided by Barry Shaw)

centuries. The letters MWP on the stone may indicate the boundary of the estates of Lord Melbourne and William Payne.

The next cross indicated along the boundary is Hartcliffe Cross and at the bottom of the map is the following note.

> *"Hartcliffe Cross-destroyed by Mr Payne and buried. Haywood a servant of Mr Firth's assisted in doing it."*

Now why should anyone want to destroy a local landmark and go to the extra trouble of burying it? The most likely explanation is that the cross was an awkward reminder of a right of way, or a disputed boundary marker. In

the *'Early History of Stocksbridge'* there is an item concerned with the ownership of the Manors of Penisale and Langsett starting with 'The Abbot and Monks, of Kirkstead in Lincolnshire, were once in possession of the Manor of Penisale, and later mentions The final separation of Midhope and Langsett Manors and their sale to Bosville and Payne.

Proceeding further west we come to Fulshaw Cross which is named but not marked by a + or drawing of a stump. Instead we have the words *"Stone marked with letter T."*

At approximately (SE175012), Bord Hill Cross is clearly marked of which no trace remains at this point today. Bord Hill Cross is shown to the west of Bord Hill Toll Bar which on the Victorian Ordnance Survey maps was close to the Dog and Partridge. Until recently there was a cross base standing at (SE18350125) next to a small enclosure near Milton Lodge, which is not shown on this map but was almost certainly the one that formerly stood on Bord Hill, unless we have the site of yet another cross. A spot of detective work by Mr Barry Shaw has revealed that this base was moved and now stands about three yards from the front door of Milton Lodge. The owner, not knowing its provenance, was considering using it as a suitable holder for plants and even of enlarging the central hole the better to house them. Here we have yet another example of how artifacts can disappear without a trace.

This stone has a square base 30 x 30 inches and tapers to 27 inches by 24 inches at the top. The mortice hole is 13 inches square and on each side of the hole there is a cross cut into the stone about 3 inches each way.

Finally we reach the summit where the Lady Cross stands. It is noteworthy that from near Penistone to the Lady Cross, the route is clearly marked as the Turnpike Road. The Turnpike Road referred to is the one constructed as a result of an Act of 1741 which provided for the road from Stockport to Saltersbrook to be continued to Doncaster through Penistone and Barnsley with a branch to Rotherham. This is the road which has milestones with Roman numerals. The map shows no trace of the New Turnpike of

Bord Hill Cross Base near Milton Lodge.
(Provided by Barry Shaw)

1830, so we can roughly date the map from this alone. The route is far older than the turnpike, and probably older than the setting up of parishes.

This map is the very thing to fuel any debate as to whether the crosses were located along the parish boundaries or the boundaries were drawn along an old route marked by the crosses. It also casts serious doubts on the cross at (SE235021) being set up as a guide for the inhabitants of Midhope or having any connection whatsoever with the Penisale Market Cross.

Pym's Chair

(SJ996767) The Rev. Charles Cox contributes the following:

> "On the high ground in Cheshire, very near the Derbyshire boundary, is a stone that goes by the name of Pym's Chair. This stone on examination proved to be the base of an early cross, one of the sides of the squared socket having been broken away giving it the appearance of a rude chair. It bears the initials PC in large capitals, on either side of a pheon (a broad barbed arrowhead). Pym's Chair

may have been a boundary marker for Macclesfield Forest."

Pym's Chair was sited at the intersection of the boundaries of Whaley Bridge, Kettleshulme and Rainow Civil Parishes, and on the route of the road from Jenkin's Chapel heading for Buxton, close to where the road north to Kettleshulme branches off. Nothing remains of this base today.

Robin Hood's Cross

(SK183803). Also known as Robin's Cross having absolutely no connection with the outlaw of Sherwood. More likely to have gained its name from Robert Archer a

Robin Hood's Cross shaft used as a stile

former lord of Abney. Referred to as early as 1317, now only the cross base remains and this was built into the bottom of a wall. The cross originally marked the junction of the parishes of Abney, Hazelbadge and Bradwell. and stood on the route of the packhorse way from Abney to Bradwell.

G.B.H. Ward writes:

> "Robin's Cross at the boundary stile where Abney-Bradwell public path leaves rough Brough Lane top is well known. It may have been fixed by the Abbots of Rufford Abbey, or another monastery and the remnants built into the wall - after the Hope (Bradwell) Enclosure Act of 1806. But I am told that a Mr Townsend broke and removed it about 15 years ago,

and used it, unknowingly, in repairing the present wall. Seth Evans in (1912) 'Bradwell, Ancient and Modern' gave an old drawing of the wall-stile, as an 'L' part of the cross and shaft, and (R) a straight length part of this possibly originally 6 feet high cross and shaft."

Seth Evans also when describing the drawing points out that the cross had a double base, but this is far from clear. The drawing from the map of 1640 shows Robin's Cross with a single shaft.

A recent examination of the site in November 2001, by Mr David Sissons discovered that there were still stones at the base of the wall which might once have been a cross base. The stile which Seth Evans described as being constructed from the cross head and shaft is still in position. The position of this cross is made slightly confusing by the way it is marked on the Dark Peak map. On a late nineteenth century 25 inch map, the site is clearly given at the point where the parish boundaries of Brough and Shatton; Abney, and Hazelbadge meet on Brough Lane at (SK183802) but the Dark Peak map would seem to give it at (SK182803) where the boundaries of Hazelbadge, Bradwell and Brough and Shatton meet. This second site is where the stile constructed from the cross shaft stands and in some ways seems the more likely site for a cross, at the brow of a ridge. The exact site of the cross will probably never be settled, but the distance between the two possible sites is such that a farmer wishing to build a stile could easily have moved the stones required.

Shuckstone Cross

The enclosure map of 1777 shows that a cross once stood at the top of the hill. The base of Shuckstone Cross stands at (SK342572) where two paths meet, and also on the boundary between Dethick, Lea and Holloway Civil Parish and Crich. It could be that there were two crosses, one at the present site and one on the hill. This base has several rather odd

Shuckstone Cross Base.

characters carved into its upper surface; some are letters of the alphabet, AELW, but others are reminiscent of mason's marks. The area has other reminders of the days of the packhorse in nearby Upper Holloway Farm and Causeway Farm.

Whibbersley Cross

South of the Big Moor lies Leash Fen which was an obstacle to travellers in the past when guide stoops and crosses must have been a great aid to chapmen, jaggers and others. Whibbersley Cross stands beside a drain which lies on the boundary between Baslow and Barlow at (SK296727). Whibbersley Cross has been rather roughly handled and thrown down in the past, but at present the shaft stands in a stone base which is visible from the road just to the north of Clod Hall Farm. Although this cross shaft stands up clear from the surrounding vegetation, it is not all that easy to pick out, which is rather unusual. I think that the colour of the stone blends rather too well with the background.

Whibbersley Cross

3 WAYSIDE CROSSES

W e have already examined a number of crosses which stand by ancient tracks and also serve as boundary markers. To the best of my knowledge the following crosses do not stand on any boundary but of course it is always possible that they once occupied a position on a boundary that has been changed over the centuries. This division is not entirely artificial and may serve the useful purpose of helping to decide whether the crosses were set up in the first instance as parish boundaries, or whether they were erected as way markers which were later used as ready made boundary markers when the parishes were established.

Before launching into a description of wayside crosses it might be as well to consider how folks found their way in remote areas before Christianity arrived in England. Existing unusually shaped hills and stones, tumuli, long lived oaks and thorn trees would all be useful and standing stones could be erected where there were no natural way markers.

Alfred Watkins in 'The Old Straight Track,' claims:

"Almost all the wayside and churchyard crosses evolved from mark stones. There is a good deal of evidence for this in some names of the wayside crosses, which are usually at crossings of old tracks."

Way markers of some type must have been in use long before Christianity reached our shores and as tracks naturally follow the best route available it would hardly be surprising if crosses used as way markers in certain places replaced existing mark stones. There is no shortage of crosses which follow old tracks in a definite direction but I have yet to come across a group which could be accurately described as standing on a "ley line," even if I were to include tumuli, stone circles and standing stones. However it could be a worthwhile exercise to examine as many standing stones as possible to see if they have been claimed for Christianity by the expedient of carving a cross on them. Standing stones are plentiful and the Ordnance Survey men go to the trouble of marking many of them on large scale maps. This raises the question of who set them up in the first place, and also why they have been left standing and not thrown down by vandals? I suspect the answer to the latter question is that they are so firmly embedded in the ground as to be beyond the ability of the average vandal to move them.

Some of the standing stones can be explained away as former gateposts left in situ when the walling stone was carted away as part of some scheme to increase field size, but there are others where such an explanation does not fit. One thing is certain, it would need a degree of organisation and skill for a group of men to move such stones into position and set them up in place. Another feature which can be seen with some of them is that the top edge is roughly chisel shaped and seems to align with some distant feature. One example is at (SK012932) at the top of the lane above Hargate Hill farm where the edge is clearly aligned with Shire Hill at (SK053945). This stone is definitely not a gatepost as it is inside the field beyond the gateposts.

Alsop-en-le-Dale

Cross Low; (SK162555) I can only give the location because this is one of the few sites I have so far failed to visit. If this was the site of a cross then it lay beside an existing footpath which joins Crosslow Lane and there is a Crosslowbank Farm nearby. This footpath would appear to follow the line of the ancient medieval Ruggeweye which went to

Pikehall. If this cross was intended as a waymarker it might have been better sited a little further north on the shoulder of the hill.

Ashtonhill Cross

(SJ983978) Stands on the route of an ancient track marked on old maps as a Roman Road leading towards Mossley from Roe Cross, near Mottram. This cross would also be a useful waymarker for travellers from south east Lancashire heading for the Longdendale Valley or the route via Edale Cross to gain access to south Yorkshire or Chesterfield.

Banner Cross

At (SK328847) near Ecclesall, is a likely site for a cross, and Ebenezer Rhodes in his *'Peak Scenery'* (1822) writes of walking the two miles from Sheffield to this feature which certainly suggests that there was a cross standing there at the time. Banner Cross is located on the old saltway from Grindleford Bridge via Ringinglow and on to Sheffield. Later this route was turnpiked and there was a tollgate erected at Banner Cross.

Beeley Cross

This wayside cross has had an interesting recent history. In the grounds of Holt House in Two Dales about a mile north-east of Darley Bridge there once stood an ancient cross-shaft. There are two differing explanations as to how the cross came to be in this position, but both follow similar lines. The first explanation is that the shaft was discovered at some date during the nineteenth century in the fields near Burley Fields Farm (SK276642) by farm workers who found it lying under two feet of earth. The owner of the land at the time was also the owner of Holt House and he had it brought there and set up on a solid base. In another account the cross was found in the 20-acre field about 600 yards north-west of Screetham Farm House near

Gladwin's Mark Farm beside Beeley Lane. This would be in the area SK299672. Either or neither of these explanations might be true; the second would lie beside the Chatsworth to Alfreton road which probably follows the same line as an earlier packhorse track, a typical site for a roadside cross, and therefore the more likely. Burdett's map shows an old track to support this suggestion and fails to show a similar track passing close to Burley Fields Farm.

Beeley Moor Cross in Bakewell Churchyard

G.H.B. Ward was in no doubt as to the original situation of the cross. On the reverse of document F17L in Sheffield Library he wrote:

> "The Saxon Cross In Holt House grounds at Darley Dale and described by T.L.Tudor in Derbyshire Archaeological Journal in 1936 was not found where stated but in the Twenty Acre Field about 600 Yards North west of Screetham Farm House and as I proved on the spot with S.O. Kay (who was told by a retired

gamekeeper). It is the first Saxon Cross which I have proved.....and came from beside the historic bridle road. It is beside the Chatsworth Alfreton bridleway as marked on this map. This history must be corrected. Possibly the owner of Holt House did not wish the site from which he obtained the cross to be known and informed Tudor wrongly."

Mr C.R. Hart discovered the base of the cross at (SK29696769) and gives a description together with a photograph in the *'Transactions of the Hunter Archaeological Society'* Vol. 17 of 1993. The base is similar to others in the area and stands 2ft high and 2ft 7ins square with chamfered corners. The sides are vertical halfway and then slope inwards to a top measuring 1ft 9ins by 1ft 7ins with a socket 5ins deep and measuring approximately 11ins by 10ins.

The Two Dales or Beeley cross now stands in Bakewell churchyard. The shaft stands five feet four inches in height and has interlaced carving with the interstices filled with small hemispheres. It has carving on all four faces and the excellent state of preservation can be put down in part to the time spent buried in the earth safe from the elements. The whole is reminiscent of the cross in Hope churchyard, partly because both are roughly square in cross-section. It would be possible to erect a complicated hypothesis concerning square cross shaft sections as against rectangular ones, but the reason might be much simpler. The masons just made the best possible use of the materials they had to hand.

This cross is not the only one in the Beeley area. In the same article by Mr C.R. Hart he describes a three-stepped, tapering, gritstone cross base which was located at SK27856844 This is close to a track across Beeley Warren which also appears to be a continuation of the track beside which the other Beeley Cross stood. The shape of this base is somewhat unusual.

Broken Cross

(SJ893736) Just over a mile and a half west from the centre of Macclesfield is a cross roads known as Broken Cross. There was formerly a toll gate at this spot and the preamble to the Act for the construction of the turnpike from Macclesfield to Buxton reads, "from the cross at Broken Cross in Macclesfield....." So the cross must have been standing in 1759.

Butterton Cross

(SK148744) A typical gritstone cross base set into a limestone drystone wall beside the old road from Tideswell to Miller's Dale. There is a gap in the wall above the base and what appears to be a well-weathered, carved portion of the shaft set above it. Looking at this base which is often filled with water, one can see why people often refer to such bases as wishing wells. The original cross probably

Butterton Cross beside old way from Tideswell to Miller's Dale

stood close to this point as it coincides with a local high point on the road and Tideswell church can be clearly seen. If crosses were deliberately located on routes between old churches then one would expect the last of a series to be placed at a point where the church came into view.

Carr House Lane

Cross cut into way marker on Carr House Lane

(SK041935) Beside the old packhorse trail known as Carr House Lane from Whitfield heading towards Doctor's Gate, is a rough standing stone with a crude but clear cross cut into it. There is no obvious reason for this standing stone, other than as a way marker, as it not a redundant gatepost. Although the cross is only a shallow mark in the stone it would have been vertical when the stone was upright which suggests that it was cut a long time ago. The stone is certainly sited correctly for a wayside cross and the stone also appears to have been roughly shaped.

Coldwell Clough

(SK055858) Turning once more to the Rev. Cox's article in the *Athenaeum* we discover the following:

> *"It may here be mentioned that the shaft of a medieval cross with chamfered edges, having the top subsequently carved into a sundial, with the date 1706 was examined by us at Coldwell Clough, on the route from Hayfield to Edale".*

This cross shaft which stood on the opposite side of the track past Coldwell Clough Farm disappeared in the late 1970s and is probably ornamenting someone's garden. It had the initials EB carved at the top, these belonging to one of the Bradburys who farmed at Coldwell Clough for centuries. This cross was certainly sited on an ancient packhorse way with the boundary between the township of Kinder and adjoining townships following the summits of Mount Famine and South Head some distance away.

Draglow Cross

Located at approximately (SK068795). Mentioned among other local crosses by William Braylesford Bunting in his book 'The Parish Church of St. Thomas Becket.' It was situated near the top of Ashbourne Lane close to the cross road from Combs to Doveholes. Apparently the house at the very top is now called "Paradise" because the new owner did not like the name Draglow; thus another reminder of our history has disappeared. Draglow Cross would be the next way marker along the track travelling north from Martinside Cross.

Dungworth Cross

(SK278903) The site only is marked on the 1906 25ins map. G.H.B. Ward describes the site as about 60 yards SE of the appropriately named Cross House, on the bank overlooking Damflask reservoir. Dungworth is only a hamlet, but was thought worthy of mention in the Domesday Survey.

Eccles Cross

Eccles Cross in Hope Churchyard

In the churchyard at Hope is the Eccles Cross which was formerly a wayside cross standing at (SK175831) where the road dips to cross the river, not far from Eccles House (SK173827). When the Rev. Cox was examining crosses in 1904 he refers to it as:

"another medieval base and part of a shaft in a field on the high ground to the south of Hope Church."

Foxlane Crosses

Foxlane Cross

There are two standing crosses near to Fox Lane at (SK294753) and (SK295748) respectively. The second of these was known as the Shepherd's Cross on the Victorian Ordnance Survey map and is now hidden from view from the road in a plantation called Shillito Wood, but the first can be made out clearly on top of a rise by the road. Before the establishment of the plantation these crosses would be in plain view of each other. The two Fox Lane Crosses are still intact but it is impossible to make out any patterns once carved

Cross in Shillito Wood along Foxlane

on them, the first of them was not improved after being mutilated by Curbar College students.

In the 1932–33 edition of the Sheffield Clarion Ramblers Booklets, G.H.B. Ward has included a map showing the site of a further cross near Foxlane at SK283744. He gives it the title of Stump Cross, which presumably is a clear description of what it once was after the top had been destroyed.

Greenway Cross

Also known as the Saxon Cross. It is a way marker standing at SJ956692 beside the route leading past Ridge Hill Farm heading for Wildboarclough over Greenway Bridge which may have replaced an earlier cross. The three crosses in West Park at Macclesfield came from Ridge Hill Farm and one can only speculate if one of them once stood at this point.

Guide Stoop opposite site of Handsome Cross

Handsome Cross

This formerly stood on Penistone Road at SK260941 on the opposite side to the existing guide stoop (Penistone 5 / Sheffield 6). It takes its name from a farmer called Hanson. Clearly sited as a waymarker visible from either direction. G.H.B. Ward adds the following information which he gleaned from the Ronksley MS.(No 1708), of John Wilson's memoranda:

> *"Ann Hawley, an old woman who lived at Broomhead in 1700, says she remembers Hanson Cross having a head and arms. The head is still there, but the arms I do not remember."*

The aforementioned John Wilson was born in 1719 and died in 1783.

King Sterndale Cross

(SK09617223). Stands on a green just beyond the hamlet of King Sterndale close to an old trackway which would have crossed the River Wye. Its continuation on the opposite side of the river is difficult to trace because of the huge quarries of the Tunstead Works. A restoration has been attempted probably when it was moved to its present position.

Right: King Sterndale 'Butter" Cross

The inscription giving details of this is almost undecipherable today due to the action of the elements. This is before yet another cross which is sometimes referred to as the Butter Cross.

Knowsley Cross

There was a local tradition current in the 1830s that Knowsley Cross once had a dial for the country people to mark the hour. This could well have taken the form of a semi-circular dial on the south face of the cross shaft with a hole above, into which a round piece of wood or metal could be inserted, similar to the one in the great cross at Bewcastle.

Knowsley Cross

Knowsley Cross which was restored in 1897 now stands at (SK103641) which is believed to be close to the original site. If the present site is not the original, then it has been well chosen, standing as it does at a high point which would be visible in both directions if it were not for the surrounding trees. The Cross is of Saxon workmanship, consisting of the lower 4ft of a shaft and a roughly hewn base which now stand on a foundation of stone steps. Although it is a Christian cross in its original shape and purpose, there is a local tradition to the effect that it marks the ninth century Battle of Longnor fought close to the boundary of Mercia, and may have witnessed the defeat of the pagan Danes. We shall meet a similar legend seven miles to the south at Ilam.

Martinside Cross

(SK07277877) A wayside cross located as usual at the highest point of an old track. This track does not coincide with a present day parish boundary, but like the Abbot's Chair was close to the line of the Roman road from Edrotalia heading for Buxton. The site is clearly marked on older 6ins maps of the district as Martinside Cross (remains of) but a careful search of the roadside and wall in June 2000 failed to find even a trace of stones which might once have served as part of a cross shaft or base. A search in winter when the herbage has died back might be more productive. Fortunately the Rev. J. Charles Cox has left us a description of the base when it was still in situ:

"Martinside Cross; the height of this squared base was 20ins and it measured at the top 28ins by 26.5ins. In the centre was an empty shaft socket 11ins by 9ins by 8ins deep. The south side of the mortise hole has been broken away, but the mortise hole is unmistakable."

The Rev. Cox also noted:

"a small channel cut from the edge of the socket to an angle of the base stone seemed to be original and may possibly have served as a pointer to the next boundary stone."

Maythorne Cross

At present this former guide stoop stands high in a field at (SE185058) where it can easily be seen from the road below. At one time it stood at a fork in the road along the old packhorse route from Thurlstone to Holmfirth at SE189057. The ancient saltway

Maythorne Cross. A new shaft mounted on an ancient base

from the Cheshire wiches which followed the Longdendale valley to Saltersbrook continued via Dunford Bridge, Carlecotes, Calf Hey Lane to the Mearthorne Cross and along Brown's Edge Road. Mearthorn over the years has become corrupted to Maythorne. It seems that there was a cross at this point long before any guide stoop was erected.

This ancient monument has been at the centre of some local excitement during AD 2000 as reported in local newspapers.

Barnsley Chronicle 27.10.2000 and *Barnsley Independent* 1.11.2000.

By Caroline Thorpe:

"An ancient boundary marker, hijacked from a neighbouring parish by Dunford residents has been given a new resting place. The Maythorne Cross will stay near Windmill Hill, Dunford where passers by can see it. The stone cross belonged to the parish of Dunford but was stolen many years ago and then found in a garden at New Mill. It was put in front of the library. When it was announced the library was to close, Kirklees council proposed to move it in front of the working men's club. That's when the Dunford residents decided to take action. A few months ago a group of locals, headed by Gerald Parker of Upper Maythorne, retrieved it with the help of a fork lift truck before anyone realised what had happened. It was taken to Gerald's farm and has now been sited on a prominent place near Windmill Hill. Kirklees Council has said it does not intend to take legal action, but says the cross should be placed in front of the club at New Mill. The New Mill Civic Society cannot afford to prosecute so it looks as though the cross will stay where it is.

Dunford Parish Council is supporting Mr Parker. Councillor Alan Prestell said the 'The cross belongs to Dunford and should never have left Maythorne. It is part of the heritage of the area and the parish council has tried on many occasions to get it returned.'"

As might be expected there is rather more to this incident than was reported in the local press. I went to see Mr Parker to get his permission to walk over his land in order to take a photograph and his first question was: *"Are you from the Council?"*

Having assured him to the contrary, he kindly showed me where the guide stoop stood originally at the fork in the road. He also has an old photograph showing it in situ to confirm this contention. The disused quarry nearby was called Maythorne Cross Quarry on a map circa 1851.

It seems that during the 19th century the guide stoop was taken by a local doctor who set it up in his garden and after his death, his relations gave it to their local council who set it up in front of the library at New Mill. When Mr Parker and his merry band collected the monument, they left a notice with the appropriate words, *"Gone Home."*

The base and the bottom section of the shaft are octagonal in shape and appear ancient, but the rest of the shaft and the capping and ball are much more recent and bear not the slightest resemblance to a Saxon cross. What we have here is a renovated guide stoop the base of which may once have supported a Saxon Cross.

Before the Councils concerned get too heated in a dispute over ownership, it might be as well to point out that the Maythorne Cross does not appear to have stood on a township boundary in the past, although it is possible that "mear thorn" meant boundary thorn in the local dialect.

Middleton by Youlgreave Cross

(SK196629) Middleton Cross stood at the crossing of the Derby to Manchester way and the Peakway at (SK196629). This section of the Peakway comes from Smerrill Grange and has the odd name of Weaddow Lane. The Derby to Manchester way approached Middleton from Elton. Both these routes are ancient and are shown on Burdett's eighteenth century map.

In the list of items in Thomas Bateman's Museum appear the following :

"(1) A Cross in the form of a quatrefoil with a rose in the centre. Found in an old wall near Middleton c 1842. (2) Shaft and base of a wayside cross; 8ft high which formerly stood near the south entrance to the village of Middleton by the Winster Road."

It would be interesting to know where these items are today. Thomas Bateman would surely have added them to his collection, much of which was placed in Weston Park Museum after his death, so they could well be amongst the ancient stones in Bakewell Church.

Middleton by Wirksworth Cross (?)

There is another site known as Middleton Cross at SK280553 north west of Wirksworth, although this might only refer to the crossroads at that point.

Mottram Sundial

(SJ994953) Outside the entrance to the churchyard stands an ornate sundial which was erected in 1897 to mark Queen Victoria's Diamond Jubilee. This was a restoration of an earlier sundial built by the schoolmaster of Mottram, Mr Wardleworth, as part of the coronation celebrations for George III. It stood a short distance from the present sundial and utilised a grindstone from Woolley Mill at Tintwistle as part of the base. This sundial in its turn replaced an older pillar which had probably been the shaft of a cross which pre-dated the church. The word pillar suggests that the original cross might have been of the Mercian type. Mottram sundial, Charlesworth cross, the Abbot's Chair and Edale cross all lie along an old packhorse route.

Mottram Sundial constructed by Mr Wardleworth

New Cross

New Cross in Bradfield Parish
(Provided by Terry Howard)

(SK218928) An odd one, which at a first glance appears to stand on an open stretch of heather moorland. However, if you stand at (SK243928) on Mortimer Road and look west over the locked gate with its barbed wire and stern warnings against trespass you will see a well defined hollow way beside the plantation which is headed almost directly for the New Cross. If you were to continue in the same direction past the New Cross you would come to the track down Abbey Brook.

In the 1926 'Clarion Ramblers Handbook' G.H.B. Ward included a map showing many features of the Upper Derwent Valley and among them was an ancient route known as Emlin Dike Road which followed this very route. Mr Ward tells us:

"According to older residents with long memories, a track once led from the top of 'Windy Lane' coming up from Low Bradfield by Agden reservoir at its junction with Strines Road, and followed west by north west by the plantation wall, leaving Emlin Dyke stream on the right, and thence to the 'New Cross', thence direct to Cartledge and Abbey Brook. This was a near cut for the Low Bradfield farmers."

Many once well used tracks were lost as a result of enclosure and the setting up of grouse moors and Emlin Dike Road is one of them. All that remains of the New Cross is a short piece of the shaft standing in a rough, well-weathered square base. The base has what appears to be a crude sword carved into it. One wonders who broke the shaft. I do not for a moment think that even the most enthusiastic Puritans would go to the trouble of climbing to such an isolated spot just for the pleasure of breaking it. A more likely explanation is that it was broken on the instructions of the landowner as part of the process of closing an old right of way. I understand that the piece of shaft has been removed recently, most likely to make the site less obvious and thus discourage walkers from inspecting it.

Why is it called the New Cross? Does it replace an older cross on the same site? It certainly doesn't look new today. The word 'new' when used to describe some antiquity in Britain needs to be treated with caution. An object might indeed have been new when Henry II rode past in 1172.

Peaslow Cross

G.H.B. Ward failed to find any physical trace of this cross. Peaslow is the south-west continuation of Rushup Edge. He came to the conclusion that the site of Peaslow Cross was near the junction of the two ancient roads which meet at a point nearly 300 yards west of the Devonshire Arms at Sparrowpit. The 25ins scale map shows the former site of Peaslow Cross at SK08668075 which confirms this opinion. Peaslow farm is about five eighths of a mile west of Sparrow Pit. The following extract from the parish registers of Chapel-en-le-Frith church confirms the existence of the Peaslow cross:

> "on 6th June 1653. Robert Newton a young man living at Congerton, killed himself at Peaslache Cross."

Peaslow and Oxlow Crosses both stood alongside a Saltway which continued down the Winnats into Castleton long before the turnpike road was made.

Robin Hood's Stoop

(SK217806) Not to be confused with the Robin Hood's Cross which is only just over two miles distant. I can do no better than quote G.H.B. Ward on the subject:

> "Every rambler should know that this ancient stoop is on the cart road and ancient bridle way from Eyam to Shatton, etc., between Highlow Hall and Offerton Hall, immediately on the left of the track and a good one third mile short, and S.E. of the latter Hall."

He then goes on to tell of the old story of how Little John was here one day before he died and he shot an arrow across the valley into Hathersage churchyard. As the distance is around a mile and a quarter I think we can treat the story with some scepticism.

However, on the subject of the Stoop he continues:

> "The present shaft is 10ins by 10ins at the bottom, and 3ft in length. The mortise hole in the base, which holds the shaft is, however, wide, and, consequently, the natives have wedged in some stone. The present shaft is probably the broken top piece and the wider bottom piece had been broken or lost. The top of the present shaft has four indents which have served to hold a top piece which I contend, has been a medieval cross."

Now here we have a little conundrum, does the word stoop refer to the shaft or the base? The shaft would undoubtedly resemble a guide stoop or signpost, but the name could also be derived from the local dialect word for a bucket or cup, or even a flagon or tankard? There is even an expression, a stoup of ale. A stoop or stoup can also be a small basin to hold holy water in church. The cross base with the shaft removed would make a fine heavy stoop. In a more religious age it is possible that water collected in a cross base was thought to have special powers and more recently for the idea of wishing wells to take hold.

Rough Lowe Cross

One of several crosses which once stood along the line of the Roman and later turnpike road from Whaley Bridge to Buxton. Having walked the route I would suggest the most likely site to have been at SK039756 where there is a mound beside the track which coincides with the highest point.

Saunder's Cross

The location of this wayside cross is perpetuated by the name Saunder's Cross House which now stands on the site at SK029977. For some reason this house is known as the Monkey House and was formerly a toll house on the Manchester to Saltersbrook turnpike road. Once more this is a site where a cross was situated on the brow of a hill beside an ancient track which was in existence long before turnpike roads were thought of. It is interesting to note that after the five crosses we have examined between Penistone and the Lady Cross we have to travel another seven and a half miles before we come across another. If there were once crosses in Longdendale then one might expect to find them along the line of the old way by Longside Edge. The Longdendale Valley has seen considerable changes since medieval times with two turnpikes, a main railway line with a long tunnel and the building of the reservoirs. Collectively these works must have hidden many antiquities, and gangs of navvies would not have been the men to show any respect to standing crosses.

Sheen

There once stood a cross at SK112615 on the opposite side of the road to Cross Farm, in the village of Sheen but by 1699 there was a house on the site of this farm.

Close to St Luke's Church in Sheen is another medieval remnant in the shape of the base of the fifteenth century village cross which has been incorporated in the restored cross that stands in St. Luke's Square.

Swire Cross

Another cross that engaged Mr Ward's attentions. He says that the late Mr Greaves Bagshawe helped fix the site of the Swire Cross near the road from Chapel to Castleton and not far from from the moor called Poor's Piece which was near the end of Chapel Gate. Chapel Gate is the name of the old track from Edale to Chapel en le Frith. He writes:

> *"I can see that Poor's Piece is the second field south-west from the top of Rushup Lane. On the north side of it is a Quarry and just north of the latter is the ancient way that goes over Breck Edge to Slack Hall."*

He also refers to a deed of 1657 in which a plot of land to the south of The Poor's Piece is bounded on its north by "a common betwixt Swire Cross and Edale...". This would appear to be about SK091824. Poor's Piece would be exactly what its name suggests a piece of common land set aside for the use as grazing land by the poor of the parish.

Summer Cross

Road leading to the Summer Cross, Tideswell

The 25ins map shows the Summer Cross at (SK14757564) near Tideswell, but the summit of this steep hill, a little further west would seem more likely. In the 'Derbyshire Archeological Journal' for 1935 Mr. T.L. Tudor gives the site of the Summer Cross as 400 yards west of Tideswell with a square base. I can find no trace of a base today but there are several pieces of gritstone built into the limestone wall by the roadside just short of the summit, and these show some signs of having once been carved despite severe weathering.

Waterfall Cross

(SK069516) Stands on the Ecton copper mine/Whiston smelter packmule route of 1770 with a Cross Lane leading to it, and at a point where five roads meet. This cross certainly lies along an old route, the Earl's Way, used by the Earl of Chester's tax gatherers.

Wheston Cross

The Wayside Cross at Wheston

(SK132764). At Wheston there is a fine ornate cross over eleven feet high in a small enclosure. One of the few crosses to have escaped mutilation, we are fortunate to have a complete cross in the area and it is remarkable that is has withstood the elements for so long. The crosshead at a first glance is similar to the one at Foolow, but surely far older. On the west face of the head is carved the Madonna and Child while on the east face is a depiction of the Crucifixion. This has to be one of the finest carved wayside crosses in Derbyshire. This cross also serves to show that crosses were not always carved on site as Wheston is in limestone country and the nearest gritstone beds are 3 miles away. Whilst still in the Tideswell area there is a Whitecross Road heading north-east from the town which indicates there was once another cross there.

Wormhill Crosses

The first of these cross bases now stands on Wind Low at (SK114752) and was probably moved from the field known as Tunstead Cross after the "Low" was excavated in the nineteenth century by Thomas Bateman; the other now lies near to the public footpath about quarter of mile NE of the church (SK127746). Both are in a reasonable state of preservation.

Cross Base on Wind Low near Wormhill

Cross Base North East of Wormhill Church

WAYSIDE CROSSES
AROUND LEEK

Here again we have examples of crosses aligned at intervals along an old route, parts of which are now hidden under a modern tarmac road.

At SJ986553, beside the A520 south of Leek stands the Plague Stone which is almost certainly the remains of a wayside cross. The carving consists of vertical fluting reminiscent of the cross in Chelmorton churchyard. Its site is where goods were exchanged for cash in time of plague. The Dipping Stone near Disley is also sometimes called the Plague Stone. Another coincidence perhaps, but these coincidences seem far too common.

About three quarters of a mile south of the Plague Stone, the A520 turns south west but if you carry on almost due south down Basford Lane to SJ988534, you will find the remains of another substantial cross stump and base at a spot called Foxdales. Still

Plague Stone. *(Photographs by C.L.M. Porter)*

Basford Lane Cross

further in the same direction you will reach the Butter Cross at SJ988523 which stands on the Staffordshire Moorlands Walk east of Cheddleton. Standing on a calvary, this cross is most impressive; the original head has been replaced, but the shaft base and calvary are all well weathered with age. All three

Butter Cross near Cheddleton.
(Photograph by R. Scholes)

aforementioned crosses are more or less in a straight line and if you follow the line in the opposite direction you will arrive at Leek Church, and less than a mile to the north of the church are the remains of a Cistercian Abbey.

Abbeys, old churches and monasteries surely have a close connection with ancient crosses.

The Cistercian Abbey of Dieulacres was founded in 1214 by Ranulph de Blundeville, Earl of Chester, possibly on the site of the former chapel of St Mary the Virgin. Various reasons have been put forward for the establishment of Dieulacres. The Abbey Chronicle states that the transfer of the monks from Poulton to Dieulacres took place particularly because of the attacks of the Welsh at whose hands they had suffered considerably. It has also been suggested that the foundation may have been a condition of the dissolution of Ranulph de Blundeville's first marriage.

Abbeys and monasteries would bring together groups of monks and lay brothers who had the skills to erect farms and build up large flocks of sheep. Left undisturbed by warring factions they would gradually amass considerable wealth. Like other religious foundations, Dieulacres was involved in the wool trade which became the main export of the land. Much of the English wool was transported to the merchants of Flanders for finishing and this would require trains of pack animals which in turn would need way markers over open moorland. For crosses to be erected for this purpose would be a natural progression for a religious establishment.

Other than castles, churches would be the only large buildings of stone in an age when virtually everyone else lived in wattle and daub huts. A monastery took years to build and would employ the masons required for that purpose. A mason capable of the fine work needed in church building would have little difficulty in turning his hand to carving a cross.

The suggestion that the crosses marked the boundaries of monastic land does not stand up to a close examination in the vast majority of cases, but there can be little doubt that a large numbers of crosses stand at strategic points along ancient ways where they would be ideally placed as way markers and also that many of these ways seem to link religious establishments.

The wealth accumulated by churches and monasteries caused dissatisfaction amongst the poor and also attracted the attention of Kings who were always short of funds to conduct wars. Henry VIII was not the first king to cast his eyes on the riches of the church, but he was the first to steal it by force. Dieulacres was dissolved in 1538.

To the north of Leek there are three or possibly four Mercian pillar crosses which also lie roughly in line. These are Heaton, Wincle Grange (now at Swythamley), Clulow and Greenway – if the last was the former site of one of the crosses at present in West Park Macclesfield.

Stilehouse Cross

Stands on Morridge at SK019567, half a mile east of Stilehouse Farm. The shaft is similar to that of the Cheddleton Butter Cross. At a first glance this cross does not appear to be on any track, however, it is situated almost exactly on a line between Butterton and Leek churches. There is also a Harvey Gate along the route, which could be a further pointer. Now there is no shortage of examples of crosses located on routes to churches; Hollins Cross and Eccles Cross near Hope church being a couple. In medieval times, long before much of the land was enclosed, it could have served as a guide to clergy and laity over what was often open moorland. If this was the reason then Stilehouse Cross could not have been visible to anyone approaching from the east, so there would be a need for another way marker at around SK025567.

An interesting feature of the tall Stilehouse cross shaft is the tenon at the top. This also occurs on a few other cross shafts which have not been broken off and would be intended to locate the missing cross-head

High Cross; along the lane between Bradnop and Onecote at SK025558 is a house marked as High Cross. Is this yet another reminder of a lost cross site?

Opposite: Stilehouse Cross *(Photograph by C.L.M. Porter)*

When Christianity came to Britain a simple cross was often carved on to existing stone monuments, to exorcise the pagan associations of the stone and to convert it to Christian use. From such simple beginnings, Christian crosses gradually became more elaborately decorated. Many early crosses would be made from wood which would soon perish. Even if the elements did not destroy them, the devout seekers after holy relics would make short work of them.

At first the stone crosses were carved on slabs, but not all the early crosses were meant to stand upright. Some were grave slabs designed to lie flat above the grave of the person commemorated. Several local churches have fine examples of very early crosses carved onto a stone slab. These are usually placed inside the porch of the south doorway and some of the best examples are to be found at Darley Dale and Bakewell with others at Hope, Taddington, Chelmorton, and Eyam. Darley Dale and Bakewell churches also have examples of stone coffins and one is immediately struck with the notion that the flat slightly tapered stone slabs bearing the inscription of the cross would fit very well as coffin lids.

Later the stones were sculpted to take the shape of a cross and in some cases the decoration became very elaborate. The walls of the south porch of the church are frequently made the last home of all the stray sepulchral and other crosses found in the surrounding district; in Derbyshire particularly it would be easy to compile a long list of such.

A much less dignified fate has overtaken many of the ancient boundary crosses and early fonts, which have been adopted as well as adapted by neighbouring farmers for agricultural uses and repairs. Every stone gatepost in a drystone wall is not a cross shaft, or cattle trough a font, but some could be and therefore warrant a closer inspection.

Churchyard crosses are usually to be found fairly close to the main south door of the church and this is the first area to look for them. Frequently, there is an upper chamber over the porch, which sometimes in the past provided accommodation for the caretaker.

In many cases you will find that the top of the cross shaft has been cut flat to accommodate a sundial and in others that a new shaft made for the sundial has been fitted onto the base of the cross. It is often assumed that these sundials were made from cross shafts which had been damaged during the Civil War period and this could well be true of many, but others look to be of more recent vintage. In the case of the sundial which stands opposite the south door of All Saint's church in Old Glossop there is a reference in the parish records to it being erected at a cost of £1 17s in 1648. The gnomen (metal rod which casts a shadow on the sundial) is now missing and the octagonal base is tilted due to the roots of a nearby sycamore tree. This sundial is typical of many others which are probably of the same vintage.

Some churchyard crosses are very ancient; older than the church itself. When the first missionaries came to England and tried to convert the Saxon villagers to Christianity, they used to erect a cross, and consecrate it, to mark the place where the people assembled to hear the new preacher and to learn its teaching. Churches would be built on the same site as the cross which in its turn may have been erected on a pagan site.

The Anglo-Saxons and Vikings built their homes from timber and the earliest churches also use the same method of construction. The very fact that they considered making permanent crosses from stone suggests that they thought them important. York Minster is built on the site of the wooden church in which Paulinus baptised King Edwin in AD

Old Glossop Sundial

to do the work and also to demonstrate the dominance of the southern English and the Catholic Church. The time at the beginning of the 10th century would appear to fit in well with this theory.

It is possible to divide crosses into different types to be found in certain areas such as the former British kingdom of Elmet, or those occupied by the Hiberno-Norse in Lancashire and Cheshire, but this is to move far beyond the bounds of the Peak.

The Normans were great church builders and pieces of stone from earlier churches were sometimes incorporated in the new buildings. In more recent renovations, ancient carved stones have frequently been set in the walls. Anglo-Saxon crosses in various states of preservation survive as standing structures or have been incorporated in the masonry of churches at Alstonfield, Bradfield, Cawthorne, Ecclesfield, Penistone, and Wirksworth to mention but a few. When looking at crosses in churchyards do not forget to have a look around the church as well. The fonts, gargoyles and other details are often well worth a closer look if only as examples of the masons' skill.

There is considerable symbolism in the construction of a church. The door on the north or "dark side" is the Devil's door which is opened during exorcism at baptism. Because entry to the church is by baptism, the font is placed close to the main door. At Communion we pass under the rood as we approach the altar signifying that heaven is reached by way of the cross. Even the long lived churchyard yews symbolise eternity. Indeed some could be so old that they were there when it was a site of pagan worship.

In writing historical articles it is common to refer to the Domesday Survey for the area. This can be a useful introduction, but because no mention is made of a church or priest in a town or village there is no reason to assume that there was not one. There are plenty of places and churches not mentioned in Domesday which must surely have existed, but it should be borne in mind that the main object of the Survey was to find how much tax could be raised.

627. The present magnificent structure was begun around AD 1230 and building continued until AD 1474, a period of time which included the reigns of nine kings.

There are obvious similarities between the rectangular shafted crosses of Derbyshire such as at Bakewell, Bradbourne and Sheffield and those of ancient Northumbria. One explanation which has been offered is that the Derbyshire crosses of this type were put up at the time when the Danelaw was being reconquered by the West Saxons and Mercians. Land at Hope and Ashford had been purchased from the Vikings for 20 lbs of gold and silver by a Northumbrian named Uhtred at the suggestion of King Edward around AD 906. Uhtred was the younger son of the English Earl of Northumbria, Eadwulf. With the fall of Viking Mercia, Uhtred was granted further lands and agreed to rule by Saxon law and custom. If Uhtred was responsible for the erection of the crosses he may well have brought masons from Northumbria

Alstonfield Church

Stump of cross on north side
of Alstonfield Church

Remnants in Alstonfield Church

that the main door is on the north side and so is the remnant of the cross. Yates's Staffordshire Map of 1775 clearly shows the lane from Milldale passing on the south side of the church and at that time, before the lane was diverted, the south entrance was used.

Ashbourne Church

Part of a cross head survives together with several stones probably of Saxon vintage in the Boothby Chapel in the north transept. The cross fragment has an unusual interlaced cord pattern which is asymmetrical. A map of c. 1537 shows a churchyard cross (P.R.O.).

In the churchyard is the plain stump of a square cross shaft standing in a square stone base. This base has the corners cut like the wayside Lady Cross. There are a number of carved stones built into the wall near the porch in Alstonfield church and numerous remnants which come from square and round shafted crosses. Many of these were found during a general restoration of the church in 1875. There are the remnants of six rectangular shafted crosses. Among the pieces of crosses found at Alstonfield are some partly carved which suggests that it was a centre for the manufacture of crosses and other religious items since it is hardly likely that anyone would transport such heavy items unless they were completed. Alstonfield Church is somewhat unusual in

Cross Arm in Ashbourne Church

Bakewell Remnants in South Porch

Bakewell Church

Opposite the east wall of the Vernon Chapel, at the Parish Church, stands the remains of Bakewell Cross. It is about 8ft in height, and almost complete except for the head. The west face of the cross is decorated with figures and the other three faces with scrolls of foliage. At the top of the north face of the cross is a representation of the crucifixion, with the soldiers with the spear and sponge on each side. The rest of the west face is divided into four panels with arched tops showing the Annunciation; a figure holding a cross over the left shoulder; a figure holding a horn in front of his body; and one which has been defaced beyond recognition. The foliage on the east face forms three bold scrolls, with bunches of grapes at each centre and leaves filling the spaces around the scrolls. At the bottom of the east face the figure of an archer can be made out shooting at a small animal near the top of the shaft, just below the

cross head. The animal appears to be holding something between its paws and to have a long tail curled over its back. It resembles a squirrel in some ways. Above this animal is the depiction of a horse trampling a figure underfoot. The north and south faces are filled with scrolls turning in alternate directions. Bakewell cross is believed to date from the seventh or eighth century. Rev. G.F. Browne identified one fragment amongst those at Bakewell (Fig 2), the proportions of which were such that it could have fitted the head of the cross in Eyam churchyard. He makes the sound suggestion that it is a remnant of the cross head of the Bakewell cross, pointing out that it is unlikely that there would have been two such ornate crosses at the one site.

Local tradition says that Bakewell Cross formerly stood at Hassop Cross Roads. If this is correct, then it is yet another example of a route marker being moved into a churchyard.

Within the south porch is a fine collection

Ornate Cross in Bakewell Churchyard (see also p.3)

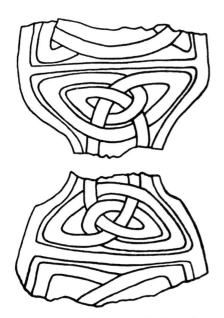

Fig 2: Front and reverse of Bakewell Cross-arm fragment

of Anglo-Saxon and early stones, some are crosses carved onto stone slabs and several which look as if they were formerly parts of a cross shaft. There is a remarkable variety in the number of different plaits and interlaced patterns. One shaft in particular is cylindrical and similar to the crosses in West Park at Macclesfield. Bakewell church has the largest collection of sculpted stones in the area, many of which are clearly portions of crosses. As Bakewell was one of the larger towns in the region with two priests to serve in the church at the time of the Domesday Survey, it could be that it was a centre for the carving of crosses for distribution to other sites.

Inside the church is another fine collection of cross shafts and other carved stones which were collected by Thomas Bateman in 1842 and later placed in Weston Park Museum, Sheffield. They were restored to All Saints, Bakewell on 25th March 1899.

There is another carved cross shaft in the churchyard which has been described in detail elsewhere (see Beeley Cross, page 40).

Baslow Church

Facing the south door of the church stand the shaft, base and steps of a cross now fitted with a sundial. Francis Bassano, the heraldic painter of Derby visited Baslow c.1710, and made the following comment:

"In the churchyard is a fair cross of five steps with a top stone and standard."

This certainly gives the impression that the cross was intact at that date. The stepped base of this cross is not typical of a wayside cross and certainly does not look old enough, being more typical of a market cross.

There is a second cross in Baslow churchyard to the left of the main entrance which was formerly located at Cross Farm in the centre of Bubnell at SK247728. Anne Tempest writing in *"Baslow 2000"* says it was moved to its present site by Doctor Wrench. There is a local tradition that this Bubnell cross was known as the "Butter Cross", which suggests that it was a convenient spot for farmers to dispose of their produce. Set into the wall of the church porch is a fragment of a carved cross.

In Baslow churchyard is the unusual tombstone of Doctor Wrench, an ex-Army surgeon who took over a medical practice in Baslow after seeing military service in the Crimea and the Indian Mutiny. It takes the form of a short column topped with a leaning cross which acts as a sundial. Doctor Wrench was responsible for the erection in 1866 of the memorial cross to the Duke of Wellington which stands on Baslow Edge.

Belper

We are now getting outside the bounds of the Peak, but close to the porch at St John's Chapel stands a cross which is worth a little examination. When the porch was added to the Chapel in 1634 the date, together with the initials of the Chapel Wardens of the time was crudely carved into the shaft of an ancient cross before it was used as the lintel for the porch. During renovations starting in 1877 the cross shaft was taken out and in 1880 it was set up in its present position with a newly cut cross head on top. The design cut into the new cross head cannot be compared with those on medieval crosses but the main interest centres on the shaft which is unornamented by any carving as were presumably the stumps of many of the wayside crosses.

St. John's was built in 1250 and the cross shaft could be considerably older. It does not have the appearance of great age, but it could have been dressed by a mason at the time the date and initials were cut.

Plain Cross at St John's Chapel Belper

Bolsterstone Church

Twin Cross Base in Bolsterstone Churchyard

In the churchyard of St. Mary's, Bolsterstone, are two large stones for which various explanations have been offered. These stones were transferred by Canon Wilson from the village green because he thought it was a more appropriate site and more likely to preserve them from the accidental wear and tear likely on a village green.

One explanation is that they were used as a medieval torture instrument for the execution of criminals. Canon Wilson, however, suggested that judging by their shape one could have been the horizontal member of a stone trabeate structure such as Druid worshippers erected at Stonehenge. He also added that the upper stone, which has a cross carved on it, was known in 1750 to have six cross carvings visible. He assumed that this was done deliberately to Christianise what had formerly been an object used in heathen worship.

A nineteenth century local historian, Wallace Charlesworth put forward a different explanation regarding these stones. He stated that they were formerly used to collect water for baptismal purposes, and were originally located at Unsliven Bridge, the name being a modern corruption of its thirteenth century name, "Unshriven Bridge." He further explained that in Anglo-Saxon times those about to accept baptism crossed the "Unshriven Bridge" entered the water to be baptised, and emerged on the opposite river bank, shriven. The stones were moved to Bolsterstone village when the bridge was widened in July 1796.

I think we can safely dismiss the notion of instruments of torture and the activities of Druids, but that there should once have been more crosses carved into the stones seems highly likely. Charlesworth's explanations have some merit because Unsliven bridge once stood at SK253992 which coincided with the junction of three townships, Hunshelf,

Penistone Rural District and Stocksbridge. The boundaries followed the course of the River Porter or Little Don, and Underbank Lane. The building of Underbank Reservoir will probably have erased any trace of a cross site. Further, many of the crosses presently situated in churchyards were brought there from outlying parts of the parish if local memories are correct. If the stone had been intended to hold water for baptism, why was so large a stone used, and why should it require two holes? Unsliven Bridge is also along the route from Bolsterstone Church to Penistone Church.

Having examined scores of ancient cross shafts and bases, I would like to offer a very different explanation. The Bolsterstones are the base of a twin-shafted Anglo-Saxon Cross, almost identical to the Dipping Stone on Whaley Moor, but in a rather better state of preservation. There are several of these twin bases and it has been suggested, without much evidence, that they were sited where three or more township boundaries met. The Bolsterstones are unusual in that if Mr Charlesworth is correct they were sited on a boundary which coincided with a river and I can think of no other example of a boundary which followed the course of a river being also marked with a cross.

Before leaving the village of Bolsterstone, there was once a wayside cross standing at SK264974 on Stone Moor Road on the way to Unsliven Bridge. The site is now occupied by a house with the name of Cross.

Bradbourne

Bradbourne is a village to the north-east of Ashbourne, (SK208528). In the churchyard close to the gate is a cross, on the lower part of which is a fine example of stone carving of the Crucifixion and interlaced foliage which has been dated to the early 8th century, but it may have been erected at the same time as Bakewell and Hope crosses. Without any written record, estimating the ages of Saxon crosses can be no more than an educated guess.

Bradbourne Churchyard Cross

When intact it must have been extremely ornate with a variety of whorls, human figures and other designs. The south face has four panels depicting figures; the upper three are too badly defaced to be made out, but the lowest depicts the Crucifixion with the soldiers holding spear and sponge and above the arms of the cross, the Sun and Moon.

On the north face are four panels, the upper two are badly worn but the lower two show two saints with books standing side by side and a saint holding a book with a bird perched on his shoulder. The other faces have ornate foliage scroll work and near the base of each, an archer shooting at men and beasts hidden amongst the foliage above.

It has already been noted that several of the ornately carved crosses depict an archer near the base of the shaft shooting at some small creature at the top which appears to be nibbling at the foliage. In the *Victoria History for Derbyshire* it has been suggested that the archer was introduced to give greater realism to the sylvan scene or more probably was intended to represent the custodian of the vineyard killing the animals and birds who are destroying the buds and fruit. If the vine is taken to represent Christ, then the archer is destroying the creatures which would injure the vine. Another suggestion is that it represents the Norse influence. The Northmen believed in Yggdrasil, the evergreen world ash which was the pathway between the gods and earth and their messenger was the squirrel Ratatosk who ran up and down the trunk perpetually whispering tidings into the ear of Woden of everything that transpired below. The little creature on the Bakewell cross resembls a squirrel clutching a nut in its paws.

The upper part of the Bradbourne shaft was for many years part of a stile which is the reason for its being so badly worn. The cross was reported as standing in 1816, but by 1833 Glover had discovered it being used as a gatepost and in 1867 the Rev. JC Cox commented on its being used as a stile.

In 1886 the piece of the cross shaft which had been split lengthwise for use as a stile post was taken out of the churchyard wall and placed on top of the standing portion so that the designs could be made out as continuous patterns. We are fortunate in that the stonemason who split the section of cross shaft managed to do such a neat piece of work so that it could afterwards be reassembled. One of the pieces of the cross which had been removed to Tissington Hall was returned at the same time. It is decorated with figures of angels and interlaced work. The restoration was carried out under the supervision of the Vicar, the Rev R.F. Borough with the approval of the Council for the Care of Churches and the Chancellor of Derby Diocese. The Society of Antiquaries defrayed the cost.

Bradbourne is one of England's "Thankful Villages". Eighteen men left the village to serve in World War I and all returned safely.

Bradfield Church

Cross inside Bradfield Church

On the north wall facing the entrance stands a cross which was found near the Cross Inn (now a private house) in Low Bradfield, marked on the 25ins map at SK263920. It was almost certainly a wayside cross. It is unusual in the area, being decorated with five balls which are a common feature of Celtic crosses and may indicate the influence of the Celtic Church through Lindisfarne.

There is an interesting local legend to the effect that the original site chosen for Bradfield church was at the point where this ancient cross stood in Low Bradfield, but that each day's work was carried away in the night to Bailey Hill until eventually the builders gave up the attempt and built the present church. Similar entertaining stories are told of other churches in various parts of England.

William de Lovetot, as Lord of the Manor of Hallam in the reign of Henry I, granted the village of Bradfield to the Knights Hospitallers of Jerusalem. Their houses were distinguished by one or more crosses displayed on the principal building. This was to indicate that the farmstead, being held by the Knights, was exempt from payment of tithes, as at Platts Farm, Ughill, where there is a cross on the north-east and south-west corbels. The sword carved into the base of the New Cross could be another indication of the Knight's past presence in Bradfield Parish.

Cawthorne Cross

The *'History of Cawthorne'* by Charles T Pratt MA (1881) contains the following piece:

"There was occasion to speak of the existence of a church at Cawthorne at the time of the Domesday Survey of 1086, the only one existing in what is now the Rural Deanery of Silkstone, and mention of it has frequently been made in connection with the various charters in which it is named. Of the early Saxon church – built of wood, probably, as most Saxon churches were – there is no trace whatever existing at the present time beyond the remains of the churchyard cross

discovered in the recent restoration, and of which there is little doubt that it dates from before the Norman Conquest. This shaft was found near the foundation of the late Chancel Arch, on the south side, built in as mere material; the cross which surmounted it, and may possibly have been an original consecrated cross of the church or churchyard was discovered over the middle pier of the north wall of the nave, hidden under many coats of whitewash.

The present church dates from the early part of the 13th century to which date may be assigned the piers and arches of the north side, though they have since been considerably altered if not altogether rebuilt, retaining their original character of structure."

Chelmorton Church

Cross in Chelmorton Churchyard

A very ancient square cross shaft stump and base standing outside the south door of the church. The remains are of a simple but unusual design. Inside the porch are two fine examples of grave slabs with incised crosses.

Grave Slabs in Porch at Darley Church

Darley Dale

Darley Dale Cross fragment housed in
Sheffield Museum

During the restoration of Darley Dale Church
in 1854 a fragment of a cross shaft was found.
The portion was 19 inches long by 15 inches
wide by 11 inches thick which suggests that
the original cross was of considerable height.
One wide face has a plait and ring pattern
which fails to match many other examples in
symmetry, and one of the narrow faces a twist

and ring pattern. (Fig 3). It is now in the
Weston Park Museum, Sheffield. Just outside
the church porch are two carved stones, the
better preserved of which carries a rectangular key pattern which is very similar to that
on one of the cross shafts at Lyme Hall near
Disley.

Inside the porch are several excellent examples of tapered grave slabs with crosses
carved onto them and outside are tapered
stone coffins.

Darley Dale church is renowned for having
the finest churchyard yew in Derbyshire. It
may well be the oldest and largest, but the one
at Monyash church is better proportioned
and merits a visit.

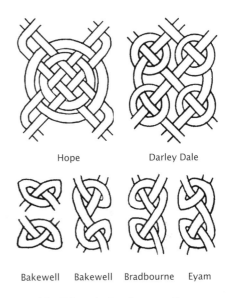

Hope   Darley Dale

Bakewell   Bakewell   Bradbourne   Eyam

Fig 3 Interlacing Patterns from
Derbyshire Crosses

Ecclesfield Church

Ecclesfield Parish once extended over a large
area with several dependent chapelries including Bradfield and Sheffield. Inside the church
is a carved stone cross shaft resting in a broken base which has two rectangular socket
holes. The remaining portion of the cross
shaft is approximately five feet high and was
probably around eight feet when complete

Carved Cross Fragments outside
Darley Church Porch

Ecclesfield Church
Twin Base

Edensor Sundial

In Edensor churchyard stands a sundial on a shaft which looks as if it were made specifically for that purpose. The base, however, looks exactly as if it were once the base of a wayside Cross. The question of where the cross once stood is not so easy to answer, because although Edensor is an ancient village with a church in Norman times, the present church and houses are of relatively recent vintage. The extensive work involved in setting up the Chatsworth Estate must also have hidden traces of old tracks and villages.

with head. The carving on the shaft is rather curious and quite unlike the work on the round shafted crosses such as the one at Leek, or the rectangular ones at Hope and Eyam. It has more in common with the fragment built into a wall at Penistone church. There are crosses in Wales with similar carving and it is possible that this is connected with the ancient British kingdom of Elmet. Both shaft and base which are made from the local sandstone were discovered during the relaying of a churchyard path near the west door of the church in 1892. The markings on the shaft can still be made out easily having been preserved in the earth.

If there is truth in the assertion that twin crosses stood at the junction of three or more boundaries then we are left with the problem of discovering where the cross stood originally. Unless of course it stood on the site of the church, which seems the most likely explanation.

Ecclesfield Parish contains several places with cross connotations, namely, Parson Cross, Burncross, a Cross Hill approached by a Roods Lane, an area known as The Cross, and a Cross House.

Edensor Sundial on Cross Base

Eyam

The cross in Eyam churchyard is in excellent condition except for the fact that the top portion of the shaft is missing. It is the only surviving example of a complete cross-head from a rectangular shafted cross in the area. From the taper on the existing shaft, the missing portion must have been about 2 feet long.

Ornate Cross in Eyam Churchyard

It stands on the south side of the church, about 8 feet in height; the base is much more recent and must have been made when the cross was set up in the churchyard. This cross was almost certainly moved into the churchyard for safe keeping, which raises the question of where it came from.

To the west of Eyam there is a Crosslow House and a cross once stood on the opposite side of the road at SK206770. Another possible site is the open piece of ground in the middle of the village opposite Eyam Hall where the stocks stand, which is still called "The Cross." Wet Withins at SK225790 on Eyam Moor, a site of pre-Christian worship, has also been put forward. The first of these three sites stands beside the road from Eyam to Foolow where one might expect to find a wayside cross, but an ornate cross like the one in the churchyard would have looked well in the centre of the village.

It might be as well to interpose a word of caution at this point. It is not unknown for locals to tell visitors what they think they want to hear. The explanation that some ancient artifact "came down off the moors", may be accurate, but a couple of hundred years ago a moor could start right at the edge of a village. Take for example Littlemoor which is within bowshot of the centre of modern Glossop.

The front of the head facing west has four angels holding sceptres on their shoulders; one is in a circle in the middle of the head and one on each of the arms. On the top of the front of the shaft are two enthroned figures in panels with arched tops; the lower figure is holding a horn in front of his body. The remainder of the front of the shaft below is decorated with circular interlaced work. On the opposite side of the head are four angels; the centre one holding a sceptre and the other three blowing trumpets. The whole of the back of the shaft is decorated with foliage, the stems of which form five bold spiral coils, with leaves and bunches of grapes in the centre of each, and leaves and buds filling up the spandrels at the sides. On the end of the north arm of the cross is a figure holding a book, and on the end of the south arm

an angel. The north and south faces of the shaft are covered with interlaced work composed of knots. Believed by some to date from the eighth century, this cross has much in common with those at Bakewell and Bradbourne.

By good fortune I possess a photograph of Eyam Cross taken in 1895 by my grandfather. Naturally the photograph is a little faded but it is still possible to make out that just over a hundred years ago the scrolls were clearer than today. One can only wonder what it looked like when it was first cut from the solid rock over a thousand years ago. The workmanship involved in carving Eyam Cross is of a far superior order to that of the much younger Edale Cross a few miles away.

In *"Highways and Byways in Derbyshire"* by J.B. Firth is the following piece concerning the cross:

> *"This is the pride of Eyam, and is nearly complete. Tradition says it was found on the moors. In the 18th century it lay neglected in a corner of the churchyard. The missing fragment of the shaft was well remembered in Rhodes' day: the sexton told him that it lay about for many years and was finally 'knocked to pieces for domestic purposes.' That the cross stands where it does is due to Howard, the prison reformer and philanthropist, who visited Eyam. It was his admiration which induced the people to get the cross set up on a new base. The chief risk to which it is now exposed is not neglect but the vandalism of the people who, during the summer months, come driving into Eyam in brake-loads. The only way to preserve it from the wantonness of those who think it sport to climb up it and sit on the arms, is to surround it by spiked iron railings."*

The word "cross" appears on the map at SK229769 to the north-east of Eyam and as it is not printed in an old script I am at a loss as to what it refers to. There is no track passing nearby nor does it lie close to a boundary. I have not yet had the opportunity to examine the area which in any case appears to be private property.

It is always the best policy to approach landowners and I have found farmers to be most helpful and they can often contribute some useful information and point out other interesting local features. Walking a few yards off a public footpath to examine an ancient cross is one thing, pulling down walls and fences or tramping through growing crops is an entirely different matter and a sure way to make problems for everyone who wants to enjoy the countryside.

On the south wall of Eyam Church is a sundial made by William Shore, a local stone mason in 1775. It is a source of wonder to watch visitors gaze at this sundial for a few moments before checking its accuracy with their watches, and finding to their amazement that it is correct.

The cross stands beside the path through the churchyard on the south side of the church and it was in this position prior to the restoration of the church in 1872. The shaft is 6 feet high of an octagonal cross-section and badly pitted due to the elements. It stands on a base mounted on three square stone steps. It is certainly much older than the 1656 inscribed on it. A plaque on the base reads:

> "AD 1897 This ancient churchyard cross was restored in loving memory of Charles Lewis Cornish Priest Vicar of this Parish 1841-46."

There is another cross built into the exterior west wall of the vestry which formerly was on the gable of the chancel. Could this be the original head of the cross in the churchyard?

Great Longstone

Great Longstone Churchyard Cross

Great Longstone crosshead in vestry wall

Hathersage

Hathersage Churchyard Cross with Sundial

Perhaps best known for Little John's Grave, Hathersage church contains a number of interesting objects worthy of a visit. Only the 4ft stump of the shaft remains standing in what appears to be the original base on the south side of the church. It carried a sundial by the local maker Daniel Rose of Derwent. In the days before folks had their own timepieces the sundial must have been invaluable, just as church clocks were to later generations. I am reminded of a friend of mine who lived in Wellgate in Old Glossop and was too poor to own a clock. (He was not alone in this, it is not all that long ago that the knocker-up plied his trade in the mill towns). To discover the correct time he had to walk to the top of the street to get a glimpse of the church clock. Inside Hathersage church are wooden crosses which once marked the graves of soldiers who fell in France in the I World War.

An unusual object at Hathersage is the Gospel Stone which is built into the base of a wall at SK236817 and on which the priest once stood to bless the crops at Rogationtide. Only one face is visible, but it well be the remains of a cross base.

Hope

There was a church and priest in Hope before the Norman Conquest and one would expect to find Saxon remains in the area. Nothing remains of the Saxon church but the shaft of a carved Saxon cross stands beside the south wall mounted in a modern square base. This cross, which is believed to date from the time of King Alfred, was hidden in the fabric of Hope School from the time of the Civil War until 1858 when it was discovered during the demolition of the old school house.

The sandstone shaft is approximately 7ft high with carvings on all four faces. The east face is divided into three panels; the upper one filled with knot work, the middle one has a pair of figures grasping a cross, while the lower has a pair of oval rings interlaced and foliage. The west face also has three panels; the upper has a figure carrying a cross over his shoulder, the centre has a pair of haloed figures embracing, and the lower is filled with interlaced work composed of double concentric rings and double cords crossing diagonally in the middle of each ring. The north face has two panels, the upper one with snakes which appear to be biting each other, and the lower filled with interlaced work founded on a four cord plait. The south face is ornamented with interlaced work composed of figure of eight knots.

The excellent state of the carving is due in some degree to the two hundred years the shaft spent buried in a wall, but the effects of todays acid rain will rapidly undo this if the stonework is not protected in some way.

Opposite the south door of the church is a calvary of five octagonal steps with a sundial pillar mounted in an octagon base on top. This base has a square hole in it which would accommodate the Saxon cross shaft and one can only surmise that it once was mounted on the calvary, although it is more typical of a market cross.

Inside the church are two burial slabs reared up near the font, with crosses, hunting horns and arrows depicted indicating that the deceased were Foresters.

Hope church was completed around 1400 and the one thing which stands out among the workmanship is the manner in which the stone slabs of the floor have been laid and remained level over the centuries. It might be a good thing if those attempting to do a similar job today were to go and study Hope church floor as a source of inspiration.

Ilam

Hope Saxon Cross set in Modern base

Ilam Churchyard Saxon Cross

In the churchyard are two very weathered Saxon crosses; one is mentioned on p.99 as an example of a Mercian cylindrical shafted cross. The other is taller and despite erosion over the centuries patterns like the ones on the better preserved crosses at Hope, Eyam, and Bakewell can be discerned.

Along the Paradise Walk by the River Manifold at (SK128505) stands a cross shaft and base which were rescued by Jesse Watts-Russell. This shaft is larger than the others but has been badly knocked about. There is a plaque beside it which reads:

> *"This cross shaft was taken from the foundations of a cottage during the rebuilding of Ilam village about 1840. Traditionally it was known as the 'Battle Stone' and associated with the struggle between the Saxons and the Danes. The carving is similar to that on the cross in Ilam churchyard."*

Leek Churchyard

Rectangular Shafted Cross
in Leek Churchyard

This contains one of the best preserved examples of a Mercian round-shafted cross, but there is another pre-Norman rectangular cross shaft with asymmetrical interlaced work in the churchyard on the south side of the church and a portion of yet another inside the church known as the Calvary Cross which has a figure carrying a cross. The cross with the rectangular shaft was set up by Sir Thomas Wardle in 1885 after its three fragments had lain for many years against the east wall of the churchyard. The existence of three crosses of widely differing appearance on the same site is the very sort of occurrence that makes it difficult to give an estimate of their ages or to come to any conclusion concerning one type of cross marking the territory of a tribal group. While it is unlikely that they all stood near the church originally, it is not unreasonable to suggest that they were brought there for safe keeping from no great distance.

The Calvary Cross, St Edward's Church, Leek

Matlock

Matlock Sundial

In the churchyard is a sundial which according to the illustrated guide to St Giles probably stands on the base of a much older medieval cross. However, the circular base with three steps is not typical of the base of a Saxon cross, being more like that of a market cross. Just outside the churchyard is Matlock Green, a piece of land belonging to the church. On the green is a large tree surrounded by a wall, and beside the wall is a rough lump of stone which is reputed to be the remains of Matlock Cross. If it is not, then one can only wonder why it has been allowed to remain there.

Remnant of Matlock Cross on Green outside St. Giles Church

Penistone

Behind the present oak partition to the west of the organ, a carved stone is set into the pillar. This is a portion of a cross laid on its side and let into a part of the wall of the church which was once the base of the original stone tower. The design carved onto the cross shaft is different to the usual foliage or plaits. It consists of squares with what might be described as letter "D"s inside. It has a lot in common with the cross stump in Ecclesfield church. There is some zig-zag Norman carving above it and a gargoyle below it.

Cross shaft built into Penistone Church

Close to the gateway in the wall on the south side of the churchyard is a square cross stump set in a rectangular base block which is almost identical to the base of the Lady Cross, Bord Hill Cross and the one near Cross Lane (SE235021). This looks like a typical wayside cross brought into the churchyard for safe keeping; its original site is a matter for conjecture, but it might well have come from Hartcliffe or Fulshaw.

In a booklet entitled '*A Further History of Penistone*', produced by the local group of the WEA appears the following item under the heading '*Crosses and Boundary Stones*':

"*Beneath the surface and near to the west door of the church is the stem of an ancient cross with a peculiar base which appears to have formed support for two cross shafts. It is rudely inscribed with characters suggestive of the Anglo-Danish work."*

Wayside Cross in Penistone Churchyard

This statement is interesting if it is correct, because it would be yet another example of a twin base on the site of an old church. Unfortunately the value of the statement is undermined by the fact that there are at least three mistakes under the same heading on the one page.

Rowsley Church

Crosshead in Rowsley Church

Propped up in a window at St Katherine's Church, Rowsley is a large fragment of a most unusual crosshead which is reputed to have been found in the River Wye and after lying in the churchyard for some years was placed inside. The remarkable feature is that the ends of the cross arms curve round until they must almost have met and one is left wondering how the sculptor managed to complete such a shape. The interlaced work on the arms is similar to that on the cross fragments found at Monyash and at present lodged in Buxton Museum. Now if this piece had been thrown into the River Wye and left there for any length of time it would surely have been tumbled along in a flood and any trace of carving obliterated, so presumably it must have been embedded in the river bank. Furthermore, the persons who overthrew the cross whether they were religious bigots, or just plain vandals, would hardly have carried it very far, so if we are to discover the original site then a search of the older roads in the area might furnish a few clues.

Burdett's eighteenth century map shows a turnpike along the route of the present A6 trunk road, but this route was chosen because the Duke of Rutland paid to have the turnpike diverted to the south side of the River Wye. The old road from Rowsley to Bakewell went past Rowsley Church before heading northwest and entering Bakewell via Coombs Road. Perhaps the cross once stood along this route as it appears to have been the most likely way to reach Bakewell Church.

Taddington

(SK142711) South of the church, between the lychgate and the church door stands a very old cross shaft 6ft high, showing chevrons and other workings which are quite unlike the usual interlaced work. Slimmer than usual and of square rather than the usual oblong cross-section, it is remarkable that it has survived so well despite having a piece missing. Perhaps its survival can be put down to the fact that it was for a time used to support a sink in the wall of a public house near the churchyard gate.

Taddington Churchyard Cross

It is sad to think that cast out fonts can end up as cattle troughs and altar slabs as bar tops in public houses but at least in some instances it has led to them being preserved after a fashion. If a cross was thrown down we can hardly blame some farmer for putting it to good use as a gatepost.

Inside the porch is a fine grave slab with a plain cross carved into it.

Tissington

Well worn cross base in Tissington Churchyard

In the churchyard, on the north side of the church, near the wall is a very badly worn cross base, but there is no trace of the shaft. The handbook produced by Tissington church says it may be a cross base. I would say it certainly is a cross base as it bears a close resemblance to several other bases in the area. It would be better placed in the correct position near the south door. The porch doorway pillars at Tissington Church also bear deep grooves from arrow sharpening, as at Thorpe.

Warslow

In the churchyard on the south side of St Lawrence's Church are part of the base and shaft of a medieval cross.

Winster

On the south side of the church, near the priest's door, stands an octagonal stone shaft with a sundial and gnomen. The base consists of three rough rectangular stones, but the shaft has all the appearance of formerly being a cross shaft which has been cut off to suit a sundial.

Winster Sundial mounted on Cross shaft

Wirksworth Church

Cross Base in Wirksworth Church

The church has a splendid collection of Saxon stones built into the walls, the most impressive being the Wirksworth Stone which was found two feet below the surface with the carving downwards when the pavement in front of the altar was being removed in 1820. Also on display is what is almost certainly the rather tall base of a cross. I know of no other like it anywhere in the region, the stepped one found on Beeley Moor being perhaps the most similar. There would appear to be two cross shafts to the side of the north porch lying on the ground.

Wormhill Church

Cross Base and Stump in Wormhill Churchyard

In Wormhill churchyard is part of a plain cross shaft on raised steps, and a sundial has been fixed on the broken shaft inscribed "The gift of Robert Meverell, gent. G.R. fecit 1670". The base is very similar to the two wayside crosses in the Wormhill area.

There is a popular notion that crosses stood on the site of present day churches as centres of worship long before churches were built. This could well be true, but in many instances there are local traditions of wayside crosses being brought down from outlying parts of the parish and set up in the churchyard to prevent further damage.

CHURCHYARD SUNDIALS

These are frequently described as being made from the broken shafts of former crosses and are also situated near the south door of the church, but many of them appear to have been made explicitly to carry a sundial.

Bradbourne Sundial

There are examples of these at Chapel-en-le-Frith, Bradbourne, Castleton and Earl Sterndale. It is of course possible that the sundial column was carved from an old cross shaft, but we already have the example of the one in Old Glossop churchyard where we know the date and cost of construction. The sundial at Castleton does not give the impression of ever having been part of a cross.

The following sundials, however, are worthy of mention as being made from cross shafts or as items of interest.

Ecclesfield

Opposite the south door of the church is a sundial mounted on a shaft, the lower portion of which looks far older than the top and on a map made at the end of the nineteenth century it was marked as a cross. The shaft is quite unlike the one inside the church. Ecclesfield church is unusual in that the nave is not aligned exactly west to east.

Mellor

Beside the path approaching the church from the east is a well weathered pillar which has borne a sundial gnomen. This pillar is very short and could be part of a cross shaft, it certainly looks old enough, but without removing it from the ground it is not possible to discover exactly how long it is. The Rev. Cox states:

> "at Mellor Church there was formerly a stone cross standing in the churchyard; it is now broken, and the remaining part serves as a pedestal for a sundial."

Despite this learned opinion it is quite unlike any portion of an ancient cross I have seen anywhere in the area. The carving at the top does not resemble in any way the vine scrolls or intertwined knotwork seen on Saxon crosses.

Mellor church is worth a visit if only to see the old, curiously carved font. The hill on which Mellor Church stands is the subject of an archaeological excavation at the present time and finds from Stone Age flints, to Iron Age pots, to Roman coins have been found so there is an excellent chance that this was once a pagan site of worship.

Unusual Sundial in Mellor Churchyard

Thorpe

Thorpe Sundial

Arrow sharpening marks in Porch of Thorpe Church

SK156502 Along the path between St Leonard's Church and the Rectory stands a tall sundial which bears the corroded inscription "Lat. 53 degrees, 00 minutes. Whithurst Derby 1767". John Whitehurst was a famous Derby clockmaker who lived from 1713 to 1788. Monyash church has a turret clock bearing the name of Whitehurst. The steps look older than the sundial column and it could well be that the original cross shaft was damaged so badly that a new one was required. Just why it is so tall is a matter for conjecture, the interesting suggestion has been made that it was for the benefit of folks on horseback. Another feature at Thorpe Church are the grooves to be found on the walls on each side of the porch doorway. These were caused by the repeated sharpening of arrow heads by local archers. A supply of bows and arrows was kept in the church for the benefit of those who could not afford their own but needed to keep up archery practice.

At (SK165505) in the garden of a Thorpe private house stands the base of the Clifton Cross from near Ashbourne, which was on the road from Ashbourne to Lichfield. It formerly stood at SK168453.

Tideswell

In the churchyard stands a sundial with an ornate shaft and base which looks much more recent than the steps on which it stands. The steps are typical of a market cross but the shaft looks as if it were made specially to carry the sundial. This sundial is reputed to mark the grave of William Newton, the so called Minstrel of the Peak. A market was granted at Tideswell, together with a fair, for two days, at the festival of the Decollation of Saint John the Baptist in 1251. The present base of the sundial could well be the former base of the market cross.

Tideswell Sundial

5 MARKET AND VILLAGE CROSSES

Village Crosses; The Cross Becoming Secularised

These were, in medieval times, generally located in the centre of villages; a sort of semi-legal position like the south porch of old parish churches where law business transactions and even marriages were conducted, as mentioned by Chaucer, and almost like the old "Pie Poudre Courts", in the open air with sanctuary to malefactors allowed. (An ancient court held in fairs and markets to administer justice in a rough and ready way to all comers from Latin *pes* a foot and *poudre*, for powder).

The village stocks were frequently placed close by, also the whipping post, and occasionally malefactors were hanged at the spot. Public proclamations were made there, and new laws declared and published, and in small villages, they became the real predecessors of the municipal and public town hall. It was the rallying place for priest and villagers on Palm Sunday when they made the procession round the churchyard into the church. The village cross and green was the focal point for celebrations during the local wakes with bull and bear baiting, wrestling, foot racing, climbing the greasy pole and similar rustic sports and pastimes.

The corpse on its way to church was set down there, that all the people attending might pray for the soul of the deceased. It was permitted for beggars to stand there when begging for alms and it even derived some respect from the popular superstition "Quersoever a cross standeth there is forgiveness of payne."

Market crosses not surprisingly do not lie on parish or township boundaries. Instead they are to be found in some central convenient position where farmers and traders could meet to exchange their wares. In many cases the date on which a market charter was granted is known, but because we have no record of a charter does not mean that there never was one. Several quiet spots today were once thriving small towns. Often market crosses, like some churchyard crosses are mounted on a calvary, or set of steps, whereas wayside and boundary crosses are usually mounted in a base stone recessed to support the cross shaft.

Ashford in the Water

Ashford Market Cross now in the churchyard

In Ashford churchyard is all that remains of the market cross which once stood on Hill Cross. It consists of three sets of octagonal steps and the base of the shaft which may date from the fifteenth century. The stone which once held the cross shaft looks very much as if it was broken when the shaft was overthrown.

Bonsall

The ancient market cross stands in the village street despite Bonsall's failure to obtain a market charter some 300 years ago. The shaft rises from a base which stands on a most impressive set of concentric steps, the number varying from eleven to fifteen due to the slope of the surrounding road surface. The dates 1678, 1769 and 1800 are cut into it and according to Bulmer's *Derbyshire* these are generally believed to refer to three restorations. Restorations of what or whom one might ask? These dates do not coincide with the commencement of the reigns of British sovereigns. The cross-head has some rather strange stone heads on it (p.18).

Buxton Market Cross in original position

find equally good reasons for doing so. The shaft is plain and of square section but has rather unusual square protuberances near the top. The base is of a similar shape to those of the wayside crosses at nearby Wormhill.

Buxton

Buxton Market Cross

The market cross in Buxton formerly stood opposite the Town Hall, but in 1949 was moved to its present position near Kwik Save supermarket. I would not like to hazard a guess as to why it was moved as both sites are now in effect car parks. Perhaps it was thought that directly outside a supermarket was the ideal situation for a market cross. I do not doubt for a moment that the council were sure they were doing the right thing in moving the cross, but would not be in the least surprised if in a few years time they decide to move it back to its original site and

Chapel-en-le-Frith

Chapel-en-le-Frith Market Cross

The cross stands at the side of the market, and is well weathered but still intact. There are faint marks cut into the shaft which some believe reads 1636. This is certainly not the date the cross was made and it looks far older. The old stocks still stand conveniently to hand for the benefit of miscreants.

Foolow Cross

The cross stands on a splendid village green. It formerly stood on a gritstone slab in front of the Wesleyan Reform Chapel and it was found necessary to move the cross when the Chapel was built. It was moved in the year 1868 and this date is marked on the plinth and on a plaque. The cross at that time was showing signs of decay due to the elements over the centuries and a new shaft was commissioned and paid for by Mr B. Bagshaw, a

Foolow Cross on the Village Green

prominent local resident. The stones which form the base today came from the original monument. The crosshead is ornate and one can only wonder at the skill and patience of the man who cut it from the solid stone. A reminder of long abandoned pursuits is the old Bull Ring which is set in the ground in front of the cross.

Glossop

Various dates have been put forward for the establishment of a market in what is now known as Old Glossop. The earliest is 1157 when Henry II gave the Manor of Glossop together with its church and lands to the Abbot of Basingwerk in North Wales. The Cistercian Abbey of Basingwerk was founded in 1131 and in 1157, Henry II granted it the manor and church of Glossop, with all its appurtenances. Lloyd's *History of Wales* says:

> "The King, Henry II on his return to Chester not only confirmed to the monks what they had previously held in Tegeingi, but gave them, out of the forfeited lands of William Peveril, of Nottingham, the vill of Glossop, in Derbyshire, as a thanks offering, it may be conjectured, for his providential escape from death in the woods of Coleshill"

Weekly markets were certainly held there from 1289 to 1833. The market cross stands in a small square near the east of the church, (SK042949). It once stood closer to the house at the east end of the square as shown in the illustration (p.17) but was moved to its present location and fitted with a new cross head in 1910. The style of the base of the cross is similar to the Lady Cross and the one in Penistone churchyard. Important national events were proclaimed at the old cross. The accession of Edward VII was proclaimed at the market cross in Old Glossop in 1901; the last monarch to be proclaimed there. The accession of George V was proclaimed at the

Town Hall in the centre of modern Glossop. The market was moved to its present position after the passing of the Market Act in 1844.

Great Longstone

Great Longstone Market Cross

The Market Cross stands on the village green; the shaft is mounted in an octagonal base which stands on a set of five circular steps. The top has been chiselled to a point. Like several other market crosses the shaft is exceptionally long.

Hadfield

There is an open area in front of Hadfield Hall which formed the original centre of Hadfield village. A hundred years ago there

Ilkeston Market Cross

The cross lies outside the area under consideration but I have included the market cross base there because although it has been badly battered over the centuries, the top of the base has circular holes cut into it which are large enough to hold coins and are reminiscent of the holes cut into the plague stones at Eyam. This appears to be a feature of several market crosses. A plate mounted on top of the base bears the following inscription:

"Base of medieval market cross which originally stood in the lower market place. This stone was presented by R.J.C. Wood Sept. 1958."

Lamp base reputed to be made from
Hadfield Cross

Ilkeston Market Cross Base

were several buildings occupying the northern end of this space but the southern portion was known as Hadfield Cross. On the opposite side of the road to the Hall is a lamp standard mounted on a stone base which is stated by some locals to be the base of the former Hadfield Cross. This base looks to be in remarkable condition for an ancient cross, but it is of the right size, fairly close to the right place, and could perhaps have been reworked by a stone mason before the lamp was mounted upon it, but I would prefer to believe it is relatively modern. Almost certainly a cross stood close by in the distant past.

Leek

Leek was granted a market as early as 1207 when King John confirmed Ranulph, Earl of Chester, a market every Wednesday in the manor of Leek and a seven day fair beginning three days before the feast of St Edward. The market cross was mentioned regularly between 1654 and 1658 as a place where banns were published. In 1671 a cross was erected at the south end of the market place by one of the Jolliffe family and it was moved to Cornhill on the Cheddleton Road in 1806 when a public hall was built on the site. In

Leek Market Cross

1857 the Cornhill site was required for the chapels of the new cemetery, and the cross was re-erected in the cemetery on a new base. It was moved back to the market place in 1986. Leek still has a thriving market and the market cross stands on a very solid base at one end. The cross is still in good condition but is not to be compared in age with its counterparts in the nearby churchyard.

Litton

Standing on the village green, this cross shaft is mounted on a square base which in turn is mounted on a set of four steps arranged like a step pyramid. The shaft itself can best be described as an obelisk and has the letters AL carved into one face and the top has been chiselled to a neat square point. These letters are neatly carved and must have had some significance at the time they were cut. Hardly the work of some northern nonentity with nothing better to do than go round defacing a local monument. Presumably there was once a cross head. Shaft base and steps are all in excellent condition and do not give an impression of great age.

Cross on the Village Green in Litton

Longnor

Beside the Warslow Road at (SK088649) close to the centre of Longnor, are the remains of what was once the market cross. The Lord of Alstonfield Manor claimed the market and fair in 1293. It was almost certainly held at Longnor. By the mid sixteenth century

Longnor was becoming a busy little place with four annual fairs and two weekly events. The tolls for the Church market were one penny for covered stalls and a halfpenny for any open stands. In 1595 the Crown granted John Harpur a Tuesday market at Longnor and by 1604 the place was of sufficient importance to have nine licensed alehouse keepers and the growing village was encroaching on the market place. Horses, wagons, and visitors would have crowded the centre of the village and the constable would find it necessary to lock up rowdies in the beehive shaped lock-up which stood on Carder Green. The present site of the market cross remnants seems unusual. Perhaps it was moved to accommodate the market hall of 1873, or one of the alehouses springing up around the village centre.

Macclesfield

According to J. Earles in *'The Streets and Houses of Old Macclesfield'*, 1915, the old market cross in Macclesfield was taken down in the year 1795 and it was either given or sold to a gentleman by the name of Mathew William Whitney, who re-erected it in a field

Monyash Market Cross

on his farm in Upton over the grave of a favourite dog. It was next taken to Weston Park and later still returned to the Market Place.

Monyash

Monyash is only a village by modern standards but in its heyday it was a busy spot. In 1340 William de Lynford obtained the grant of a weekly market on Tuesdays, and a three days' fair at the festival of the Holy Trinity. This market was granted to encourage the development of the lead mining industry. The market is no more but the market cross shaft still stands on a base mounted on a large square step which is reputed to be made from the old stocks. Its position on the green would be an ideal site for a village market. The base also has circular holes cut into it like the ones at Ilkeston and elsewhere.

Penistone Market Cross

Inside the churchyard at St John the Baptist's at Penistone can be seen the base of a cross of good design which is used as the base of a flagpole. This base formerly stood outside the churchyard on the site of the present War Memorial and is all that remains of the old market cross.

Wirksworth

In 1307, Thomas, Earl of Lancaster obtained a grant of a weekly market. The market cross shaft stands in the churchyard on the north west side, rising to a height of nine feet. The shaft is plain and there is no trace of the cross head. The base is a large square stone block. The shaft has been dated to the thirteenth century and is thought to have been brought into the churchyard during the late eighteenth or early nineteenth centuries for safe keeping.

Youlgreave

Opposite the south porch on the steps of the old village cross, which were moved to the churchyard in the early 19th century (?1829) from Fountain Square, stands a sundial of 1752 mounted on a large upturned font. There is no trace of the cross shaft. Youlgreave church is well worth a visit if only to study the different styles of architecture and its fine alabaster carvings.

Left: Wirksworth Market Cross shaft and base in the Churchyard

Below: Upturned Font mounted on the steps of Youlgreave Market Cross

6 MEMORIAL CROSSES

These come in a very different category to the crosses we have come across so far but are worthy of mention as reminders of various events in our history during the last 200 years.

Ashway Cross

Ilam

Ashway Cross

(SE031045). Overlooking Dove Stone and Yeoman Hey Reservoirs is a memorial cross to the accidental shooting of James Platt, who was the MP for Oldham. This tragedy occurred while on a grouse shoot in 1857. The keepers and beaters carried him down to Ashway Gap House which belonged to his brother but he died two days later. Because of the strong winds which scour this remote spot it has become necessary to support the cross with steel rods. The Platts were famous as manufacturers of textile machinery in Oldham.

Eleanor Style Cross at Ilam

In the village of Ilam is the unusual and elaborate cross erected in 1840 by Jesse Watts-Russell in honour of his wife. It is built in the style of the Eleanor crosses erected by Edward I. It is becoming badly eroded.

Stoney Middleton

Corn Laws Cross, Stoney Middleton

Here stands a very solid looking cross sited across the road from the Moon Inn inscribed with the date 1846. The story behind the erection of this cross is somewhat unusual. It does not commemorate some great military victory or war hero, instead it was erected to celebrate the repeal of the Corn Laws in 1846, an event which was of far greater importance and benefit to working folks.

Another political event recorded three miles south of Stoney Middleton was the passing of the Reform Bill in 1832, the previous rejection of which caused riots in Derby and elsewhere. The so called Reform Stone is still marked on maps at SK213807, but at best seems to have been no more than a pile of stones. It certainly was not a cross.

Wellington's Cross

The cross set up on Baslow Edge by Doctor Wrench in 1866 as a balance to the Nelson monument on the hill opposite and also to record a visit by the Iron Duke to the moor as a guest of the Duke of Rutland. It stands atop a massive block of Millstone Grit and is constructed from individual stones instead of being cut from one piece. It can be clearly made out from the Baslow to Sheffield Road below, see page 16.

THE CROSS AS A WAR MEMORIAL

In many villages the War Memorial to the fallen in the Great War takes the form of a cross. I have chosen the one in Hollingworth as a typical example of those erected during the 1920s. There are few local folk who cannot see the name of some relation among the names of the fallen. For some years after the erection of these memorials, men would raise their hats as they passed; after all these were memorials to men with whom they had shared their school days and working lives.

The Hollingworth War Memorial is exceptional in that Tony Catchpole has gone to immense trouble to trace the history of this cross. He has researched the background of the Council deliberations before the Memorial was erected and the personal details of all the fallen and compiled them into a book entitled *A Simple Cross of Cornish Granite*.

Yet another is the cross erected in the early nineteen twenties in the upper Derwent Valley overlooking the now submerged village of Derwent, as a memorial to the men of the valley who fell in the First World War.

There is something very poignant about reading the names of the fallen; many with surnames of families which had dwelt in the area for centuries and some even giving their names to farms now demolished. In 1891 there were Cottrills at Gores farm; Eyres at Alport and Marebottom farms; Thorpes at Wellhead. From the Record of Baptisms at Derwent Chapel we find that there was a

Derwent War Memorial

William Thorpe Miller and Farmer living at Mill House situated on the Mill Brook from 1844 to 1874.

Pte	George Cottrill	KRR.
Pte	Arthur Dakin	Notts & Derby Regt
Corp	George Dunn	Yorks & Lancs Regt
Pte	Wilfred Eyre	Yorks & Lancs Regt
Pte	Walter Heathcote	Yorks & Lancs Regt
Gds	David Kennedy	Grenadier Guards
Pte	Jason Priestley	Notts & Derby Regt
Gds	Gregory Thorpe	Grenadier Guards
Pte	John Wilson	Notts & Derby Regt
Drv	John Joseph Thorpe	RFA

Derwent War Memorial

Hollingworth War Memorial

As you stand there reading their names, try to imagine for a moment living in a beautiful quiet rural backwater like Derwent and then being suddenly transported into the hell of trench warfare. This cross was carved by Arthur Dane, an Eyam stonemason. We often know the names of local benefactors who paid for the building of churches, fountains and schools, so it makes a pleasant change to know the name of the man who actually did the work.

Cross shafts can be of various cross-sections, usually square or rectangular and sometimes octagonal. Round cross shafts of a distinctive type are to be found in Staffordshire, Cheshire and the High Peak of Derbyshire. They are often referred to as Mercian Pillar Crosses but are almost entirely restricted to that part of Mercia north of the River Trent. One exception to this is a round shafted cross at Gilling West which is about 3 miles NNE of Richmond in the North Riding of Yorkshire. Apart from this, the area where most are to be found also coincides with the district once inhabited by a tribal group known as the Pecsaetna, from whom the Peak District takes its name. (Map 4) These crosses have round shafts with a curving taper which usually ends in a single or double roll surmounted by a tapered square sculpted section which is topped by the cross head. None of these crosses survive in the complete state but from examining the remnants it is possible to make a fair estimate of their original appearance. The following is a list of the Mercian type crosses which have so far been found, listed under the counties in which they stand:

DERBYSHIRE

Bakewell

In the south porch at Bakewell church there is a fine collection of early carved stones which include a number of cross shafts, bosses and arms. The fact that there are so many found at Bakewell during excavations at the church suggests that Bakewell was a centre where crosses were made and distributed through the area. Several of these shaft sections are very similar to those at Lyme Hall and there are several cylindrical sections which certainly come from Mercian type shafts. There is one particular piece which has part of the round section of the shaft, the double collar and part of the square section similar to those at Macclesfield and Leek.

Twin Mercian Pillar crosses (How the Picking Rods might have looked originally)

Robin Hood's Picking Rods

(SK006909) The subject of controversy in the past and to this day as to their origin. Romantic tales of Robin Hood stringing his bow with their aid and shooting an arrow from that point using the Mare's Back about a mile away as his butts can be dismissed as flights of pure fancy as can anything associated with

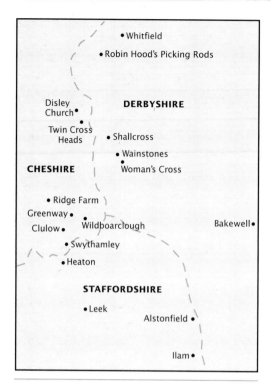

Map 4: Distribution of Mercian Pillar Crosses

druids, fairies, and UFOs. These ancient stones stand at the junction of the Township boundaries of Ludworth, Mellor and Thornset and close to the boundary of Chisworth, and also on the route of an old track. In the area of the Picking Rods the ground is quite waterlogged, but there are traces of metalling having been laid down, so this track may once have been of greater importance. Before the Glossop to Marple Turnpike was made in 1803, this would be a main route from Glossop to Ludworth. Certainly in the mid nineteenth century when Besom Sam Higginbottom lived at Far Slacks Farm, his wife Martha would walk regularly to Glossop market with a baby on one arm and a basket of eggs on the other using the track passing the Picking Rods and going over Coombs, Duns Clough and Chunal. For some reason which I cannot explain Duns Clough is not named on the map but is pronounced Duns Clews. The section of this track which runs past Plainsteads Farm was once a popular walk and in far better condition than it is today.

The moor on which Robin Hood's Picking Rods stand was first enclosed in 1676 and there is a record of 1791 which states that the two stones were lying on the ground beside their sockets. At some later date the two stone pillars were replaced in their sockets and roughly secured by wooden wedges. Having again become loosened they were secured and cemented round the bases by the Hayfield Antiquarian Society, and were subsequently protected by an iron railing erected by Lord Howard of Glossop. No trace of this railing exists today. The base into which these two stones are mounted is a stone 2ft thick and measuring 6ft 10ins in length and 4ft 1ins in breadth. Both shafts have been mutilated and are without any trace of the heads which, if they are of the usual type of Mercian round-shafted cross, they certainly once had. The distance between the circular sockets is 12ins. The taller of the shafts has a diameter of 19ins and stands 3ft 9ins above the base. The other has a diameter of 21ins and a height of 2ft 6ins. A piece of the shorter shaft some 2ft 3ins long is built into one of the nearby walls. The base is also marked with a letter N. When complete the Picking Rods must have been an impressive sight. After examining so many of these crosses in the area I think it can be stated with complete confidence that the Robin Hood's Picking Rods are the remains of what was once a fine example of a double shafted Mercian cross.

The Shallcross

Around 1904 a cross shaft was discovered by W.J. Andrew, FSA in the grounds of Fernilee Hall (SK015786), where it had been converted into a pillar used to mount a sundial. Local tradition was that this cross shaft was brought from its original site to Fernilee Hall around 1800. The upper part was clearly a section of a round shafted, cross shaft having a double collar at the top of the cylindrical portion, topped by a truncated square section which showed some signs of carving, very similar to the ones at Macclesfield. The shaft is about about five feet long of which the

The Shallcross near Whaley Bridge

double collar and square top section take up a 1ft. The girth at the foot of the column is 35ins tapering to 32ins below the collars. On each of the square faces is a moulding in the form of a staple and on one of them the initials HL above the date 1720 neatly carved.

This staple shape has led to some learned theories being expounded to the effect that the shape is a shackle and hence the name was once Shacklecross which became corrupted to Shallcross. An examination of several others of this type of cross is sufficient to nullify this suggestion.

Fernilee Hall is around five miles north west of Buxton and is less than half a mile west of the route of the Roman Road from Buxton to Manchester. Maps of the area circa 1640 show that along this stretch of road there was a series of crosses; Rough Lowe Cross, Woman's Cross, Wainstones Cross, and Shallcross. (Map 4). It is a reasonable assumption that the shaft of one of these crosses ended up at Fernilee Hall, but which? Rough Lowe Cross was the nearest to Buxton, and I have suggested a possible site in the chapter on wayside crosses (p.51).

There is some guidance to be obtained from Marguerite A Bellhouse in an article entitled "Lost Woman's Cross in Combs Edge" in 'Derbyshire Miscellany', and also from Mr W.B. Bunting in his book on Chapel-en-le-Frith.

The Woman's Cross (Weeping or Lady's Cross)

The cross would appear to have stood at SK034764 where an old track comes up from Combs Hollow and Chapel-en-le-Frith. Mr Bunting writes that it is marked on old maps at White Hall which would be a natural site at the meeting of two bridleways. At one time outside the rear gate of White Hall was a large square stone, with a hole in the top which could well have been the base of the Woman's Cross.

Marguerite Bellhouse contributes the following interesting details, some obviously unearthed by the sound method of getting about and talking to older local folk:

"The earliest record of the Woman's or Weeping Cross at Combs Edge is a map of 1640, when it is shown standing at the corner of the trackway to Combs, adjoining the old coaching road from Buxton to Whaley Bridge, and on the Archer's Wall which was the parish boundary. (The Archer's Wall is an ancient one which separates the moors from the fields below). It is again shown on W Marsland's map of 1707, but since it has disappeared.

It is mentioned in the Reliquary as a penitent's cross, built into the Archer's Wall, and it is also mentioned by W B Bunting on pp 16-17 of his book on Chapel-en-le-Frith.

The account in the Reliquary of the Woman's Cross states that from its position one could see Kinder, Cheshire and the Yorkshire hills, and this points to the position at the corner of the Combs track. Another old resident, Mrs M Thorniley, told the writer that 50 or 60 years ago a long rounded stone lay in the field called Upper Peat Knowle at the junction of the Combs track from Whitehall and that she and her sister rolled it down the steep field towards the clough, belonging to Hazelhurst Farm, where it remained.

While walking by way of Baghouse Flatt and Strawberry Bank on 28 February 1972, the writer glanced over the wall into the corner of Upper Stoney Knowle Meadow and saw two stone rollers with a rotted wooden frame which must have been there a long while. One was of a very rough gritstone almost circular and very clearly a roller, but the other was quite different being of a smooth sandstone bearing the patina of years of weathering. This stone was 48 inches long and oval not round in shape, tapering slightly to the top. At the base was a small rough cross mark and near the top was an oval mark, now obliterated, which appears to have some sign or letters within. Mr Jacob Lomas who owns the farm and

has lived there for 80 years, realises that the two stones are different but says that they have been there as long as he can remember. Both have irons cemented into their ends to facilitate rolling operations."

The details given in this account show that the Woman's Cross had a round shaft, but if it ended up as a stone roller on a farm after being rolled down a steep hillside it cannot be the one at Fernilee Hall.

Wainstones

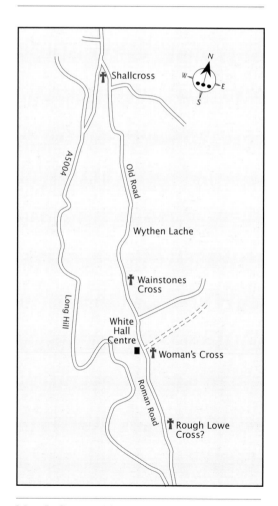

Map 5: Crosses Along the Whaley Bridge to Buxton Turnpike

The cross stands at SK028771 on the boundary between the civil parishes of Whaley Bridge and Chapel-en-le-Frith about 1.25 miles from Fernilee Hall. The cross would not be far from this site which also happens to be a high point visible from both directions. Marguerite Bellhouse says that a large squared stone, with a circular hole in it which could be a cross base was dug up in 1965 at Wainstone, and still lies at the roadside. Also according to a late resident of Withen Lache, the base of a cross once stood near Wainstones and part of a cross head lay half buried in the grass at the Windgap where it was used to tether packhorses. The writer discovered the latter, but it was moved before it could be saved. Now if this circular hole matches the Fernilee Shaft we might have the solution.

Note that we have two crosses set in circular sockets which strongly suggests that they were of the round shafted Mercian type.

This leaves us with the Shallcross. On the 2.5 inch Ordnance Survey map we have Cross (remains of). Now sometimes we might fault the Ordnance Survey for omitting a place of interest, but they can hardly be accused of showing a feature that does not exist. This would be a suitable site, located at a fork in the road, and although not on an existing boundary, it is possible that the boundary has been altered in the past. Before making an angle at SK025793 the boundary was headed directly towards this site. At the time of its discovery, Mr Andrew was of the opinion that the Fernilee cross had come from this point.

If the letters H.L. 1720 carved into the Shallcross are really due to a survey in that year, and the same applies to other crosses similarly marked, it strongly suggests that the Shallcross was in situ on the road above at that date.

In 1675, John Ogilby produced a book of the main roads in England at the express desire of Charles II. The roads were shown by a series of strip maps with principal features along the route. On the north side of the old road from Manchester to Derby, just south of "Shawcross Hall" (his spelling), is an illustration of a cross atop a hill. This would coincide with the position given on a modern map.

Ogilby does not show any of the other crosses which suggests that they had been thrown down during the English Civil War.

This is not the only possible explanation. Mr Bunting referring to a cross now in the garden of Fernilee Hall, says it is not clear whether it was originally there or at the side of the road up Elnor Lane – about one mile from Shallcross Hall, between Whaley Bridge and White Hall, now called the "Old Road". This, although not proven may be the original site of Shallcross, near a bridle roads meet. This would be at around SK022788. Mr Bunting elsewhere says that Fernilee Cross was built in a wall not far from Wythen Lache Farm. The site may have been near the junction of the ancient road with the old track coming SSW from Thorny Lee Farm at the south end of Long Edge Plantation. This would be at (SK026776) which is about three quarters of a mile from his first suggestion. We shall probably never know exactly where along the line of the old road the Shallcross came from but wherever the true original site, the remains of the Shallcross now stand at SK01637965 within a small stone enclosure. A much newer, shaped piece of stone has been cemented on top for some reason. It looks rather odd but might be intended to protect the top of the shaft from the worst of the weather.

Whitfield Cross

There are other less well known examples of round shafted crosses in the area. The well worn stump of Whitfield Cross now forms part of a stile on the footpath from Carr House Lane to Cross Cliffe (SK041937). I wonder why none of the antiquarians seem to have made reference to it. Perhaps they were aware of the ancient practice in Whitfield Township of local youths throwing strangers into the wells and consequently avoided the area. The top of the shaft is shaped rather like the tops of the Bow Stones near Disley. The cross originally stood at the top of the area known as Whitfield Cross where it would be beside an old packhorse

Whitfield Cross, now part of a stile

route from Hayfield which turned off near the bottom of Chunal passing through Gnathole, Whitfield Green, along Hague Street and down the appropriately named Cross Cliff to what is now known as Old Glossop.

There are several large stones built into a wall there which could have formed the base of the cross. The cross shaft was carried off by a gang of lads from nearby Cross Cliffe as a "Mischief Night" prank around 1800 and never replaced. John Nelson, one of John Wesley's assistants, preached at Whitfield Cross at some date prior to his death in 1774.

Brailsford Cross

At some distance from the Peak but mentioned because it is another example of a Mercian type cross within the county. The cylindrical portion of the shaft is shorter than usual and could best be described as barrel shaped as it tapers in both directions. The shaft is also

different in having a figure wielding a drawn sword below the twin collars. The remaining squared portion at the top is filled with the usual plaits and key patterns.

STAFFORDSHIRE

Alstonfield Churchyard

We have already visited Alstonfield Church and seen the stump of a square shafted cross mounted in a plain base and the fragments of square and round shafted crosses inside the church. There are more examples of Saxon crosses in Alstonfield churchyard than anywhere else in Staffordshire. An examination of these fragments reveals that there are at least four pieces of Mercian type shafts because they show the section where the round portion merges into the square below the head and this can only occur once on each shaft.

Alstonfield Mercian Cross Shaft used as a Sundial

Moreover, on the south side of the church is a sundial mounted on a round shaft which has been rather crudely cut to a square section at the top. This shaft is now only 39ins in height and 48ins in circumference, but one glance is enough to identify this round shaft as that of a Mercian Cross.

Heaton

At SJ952627 north east of Heaton hamlet stands part of an Anglo-Saxon cross with a circular shaft.

Ilam

In the churchyard at Ilam in Staffordshire are two crosses. The smaller of these which may have lost the lower part of the shaft is yet another example of a cross with a round shaft

Ilam Mercian Style Cross

surmounted with a single collar and a square carved section plus the central boss of a cross head. It is smaller than the other examples standing only 51ins and no more than 42ins in circumference. When around 1890 Prof. G.F. Browne dug round it, he found that the shaft was let into a rude stone socket with lead. It has suffered badly from the elements but some of the carving can be made out and it still resembles the other pillar crosses.

Leek Churchyard

To get a better idea of what these cylindrical shafted crosses must have looked like when first cut from the sandstone, take a trip to the Parish Church of St Edward at Leek and examine the single example in the churchyard. The base is comparatively recent but the shaft is almost complete. The cylindrical portion of the shaft measures 67ins at its greatest circumference and 77ins in height. When the complete head was in place, the perfect cross must have been more than 11ft in height. The elements have certainly worn the stone away, but the central boss of the cross head is still in place and you have only to imagine the arms to know how it must once have appeared. This cross shaft differs from the others we have examined in that the collar has been sculpted with interlacing and there are patterns of knotwork on the four faces of the shaft just below the collar. The squared portion of the shaft is carved in a manner very like the cross heads at Lyme Hall.

Another odd historical feature of this cross is that it also bears the marks of bullets fired during the 1745 rebellion. There is seemingly no end to acts of senseless vandalism.

Before leaving Staffordshire it should be pointed out that there are further round shafted crosses at Chebsey some eight miles south of Stoke on Trent and another which was found in Stoke on Trent churchyard in 1876 when the sexton was digging a grave. However, we can hardly claim these as being within the Peak.

Many crosses are ornamented with an interlaced pattern of Staffordshire knots. Just

The splendid Mercian Cross shaft in
St Edward's Churchyard, Leek

how did this knot become a Staffordshire
emblem? Could it be from these ancient cross
patterns?

CHESHIRE

Clulow Cross

(SJ953674) Stands near the point where the Congleton–Buxton and Macclesfield–Wincle roads cross and near the boundary of the townships of Wincle and Sutton. At present it lies half hidden in a small plantation but previously it would have stood out as a way marker on a mound. It has a large cylindrical shaft nearly 7 feet in height with two fillets and the portion of the squared shaft below the head. It no longer stands on a route, but once the medieval holloway between Leek and Macclesfield passed close by.

Clulow Cross

Macclesfield

The Three Mercian Cross Shafts in
West Park, Macclesfield

In the West Park at Macclesfield in the children's play area are three Anglo-Saxon cylindrical shafted crosses. The heads have been broken off, but sufficient remains to see that the top was of a square section surmounting a double collar. They are very similar to the Bow Stones but have retained a larger portion of the squared section. These three cross shafts were brought from Ridge Hill Farm at SJ934711 to the south of Macclesfield. This information immediately poses the question, what were three crosses doing on one farm and how did they get there? One pointer is that Ridge Hall Farm lies on an old track and that the Greenway cross stands a couple of miles away on the same route. Perhaps some farmer recognised the value of these relics and collected them together out of harm's way. Two of them are reputed to have been originally at Greenway and Wildboarclough which could be accurate since both places lie on old tracks.

Swythamley Cross

Although it now stands in Staffordshire, this cross really belongs to Cheshire because around 1874, the squire of Swythamley removed it from the yard north east of Wincle Grange (SJ956654) in the parish of Prestbury to its present position in Swythamley Park at SJ970648. There appears to be no pattern carved into the square portion of the shaft but it has two circular fillets. A small modern cross has been added to the top which looks rather out of place. Wincle Grange stands beside the medieval route from Leek to Macclesfield.

Still in Cheshire, but moving well away from the Peak District there is another cross similar to Clulow and Swythamley crosses, near Upton Hall on the Road from Macclesfield to Alderley Edge.

Mercian Crosses at Disley

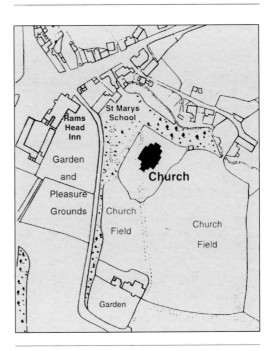

Map 6: Section of the Tithe Map for Disley showing the Church Field

There are plenty of references to twin Saxon crosses which once stood on the present site of St Mary's Church Disley, or close to it. Despite this plethora of information it has been extremely difficult to establish any firm facts because much of what has been written is contradictory and in some cases misleading at best.

From the facts so far ascertained the following would seem the most likely scenario. The twin crosses were set up in a single stone base close to the present site of St Mary's Church in Anglian times before any church was built. They would be thrown down around 1548 as part of the religious upheavals during the reign of Edward VI and left where children no doubt climbed over them until eventually they were covered with earth and vegetation and forgotten. These remnants might have been lost to us but sometime in the seventeenth century two round shafts were found in the Church Field (Map 6), and were claimed by the Leghs

Swythamley Cross

of Lyme who set them up in a specially made stone base sunk into the ground on the boundary of their estate at SJ973813. Where we know them today as the Bowstones.

One odd fact that has emerged is that in 1465 a feature known as the Borestone is mentioned in a Legh Terrier. This Borestone appears to have stood at or near the present site of the Bowstones. The date is too early for it to be one of the Bowstones but it could have been a standing stone used as a way or boundary marker. The Borestone might be totally unconnected with the Bowstones but its name could easily have become Bowstones over a period of time if they were used to replace it.

By 1793, in the Torrington Diaries, Byng mentions "the pillars" where the Bowstones now stand and in the *'Antiquities of Lyme'* of 1810, Marriott refers again to "the pillars". These pillars are typical Mercian Pillar shafts. Bowstones is an odd name which could be behind the ludicrous story of Robin Hood stringing his bow at the Picking Rods. The fact that two parish boundaries head for the present site of the Bowstones and then turn away as noted by the Rev. Cox is most likely a pure coincidence. The age of the track they stand alongside might be of greater relevance. For the Leghs to claim the shafts is just another example of a Lord of the Manor, or member of the gentry acting normally, but at least it has led to these artifacts being preserved intact when they might easily have been broken up or incorporated in some building.

So far, so good, the base in which the Bowstones are now set in no way resembles the base of a Mercian twin cross, or any other ancient cross. The Bowstones do resemble other Mercian crosses in having a circular shaft with a single collar and above this collar approximately six inches of the squared carved portion remains. It will be necessary to return to this squared portion later.

The next event in chronological order occurred around 1840 with the discovery of twin cross-heads. It is at this stage confusion enters the story. In one account the cross-heads were found in the Church Field like the Bowstones; in the other, they were found at a spot called Badger Clough. The suggestion that the cross-heads were found in the Church Field comes from a report in the *'Archaeological Journal'* of 1848 which would also have us believe that they had once been grave crosses which they certainly were not. The Badger Clough site is much more likely and there is a clear account in the *'Manchester City News'* of 31/5/1890 by Mr Isaac Watt Boulton of how the cross-heads were found at Black Farm at the north end of Whaley Moor which is about a mile and a quarter SE of Disley Church. We must leave these cross-heads for the moment as they will be dealt with separately later.

The following piece of information comes as an extract from the booklet produced for St Mary's Church, Disley:

"The old font, a large sandstone bowl, unornamented, was recovered in 1958 from beside the spring in the Vicarage field. At the same time a large block of sandstone, roughly rectangular and with two large holes cut in it, was dug up near it. This discovery is naturally linked with that of the two sandstone crosses which are based at Lyme Hall and which, according to an account in the Archaeological Journal of 1848, were 'ploughed up in a field near the church of Disley.....and removed to High Lane by the late Richard Orford.' From here they were taken to Lyme Hall for safe keeping. These crosses have been identified as twin crosses of Anglo-Saxon work of the ninth or tenth century, and the measurements and general appearance of the large block of stone are what one would have expected of the presumed single base for the Lyme Hall crosses....and the site of the discovery is sufficient confirmation for the view that the Lyme Hall crosses stood as a pair, near the site of Disley Church, in the century before the Norman Conquest."

Leaving aside the old font, this is a statement remarkable for its failure to report the find accurately and for jumping to conclusions on the scantiest of evidence. What a pity

The Bow Stones from Disley Church

the Rev. Cox was not on hand to give an account of the stone base. He would certainly have apprised us of the dimensions and any special features. The most glaring omission is the failure to state whether the holes in the stone were round or rectangular. The only possible reason for stating that the twin cross-heads had come from Disley Church is that they are of the type associated with Mercian Pillar shafts. It appears that the Vicar of Disley at the time made unsuccessful attempts to have the component parts reassembled in the churchyard. It is perhaps, to be regretted that he did not succeed, then we would know for sure if the various parts matched, instead of such unsubstantiated statements as:

"The Bowstone shafts, two cross heads, and the newly found plinth were obviously the complete remains of a twin round shafted Mercian cross."

Where is the stone today? What shape and size are the holes? Would the Bowstone shafts fit into them? Would the Cross-heads fit on top of the Bowstones? These are the sort of question to be asked by serious researchers.

Firstly the twin stone base. Having read an account of its being in Disley Churchyard I commenced my search there but could find no trace. Now a stone of this size is hardly likely to be carried away in someone's car boot as a garden ornament, and yet no one seemed to know where it was. At one stage I was beginning to wonder if the account in the Church History was a flight of the imagination. After two and half years of persistent searching I can tell you that it stands near the wall of the car park outside Disley Church-yard, and it has two round holes capable of accommodating Mercian style cross shafts.

The stone base is 6ft long and tapers in width from 3ft 6ins at one end to 2ft 6ins at the other and is just over a foot deep. It has two circular holes, the larger one being approximately 19ins in diameter and the smaller 18ins. The Bowstones by comparison are 16.5ins and 16ins respectively in diameter at their bases so they would have fitted into the base, if somewhat loosely. The portion of the Bowstones sunk in the present base would be larger and result in a better fit. Mercian pillar shafts come in a variety of sizes and therefore it is a perfectly reasonable assumption that the Bow Stones once stood in this base 450 years ago.

The Twin Cross-Heads from Whaley Moor

The following piece was written by G.H.B. Ward and appeared in the annual booklet of the Sheffield Clarion Ramblers. Mr Ward also went to the trouble of inspecting the site and talking to local folks; always a sound policy.
'*Two Unknown Crosses and the Lyme Park Crosses*':

"*Mr Isaac Watt Boulton, a late, virile Ashton-under-Lyne antiquarian and eminent Victorian engineer, in the Manchester City News of 31/5/1890 described two ancient crosses which now in Lyme Park should be national monuments and if possible to locate them, be fixed as near as may be to the original sites. They are perhaps the finest pieces of antiquity in the district and remarkably similar to one found on the Trafford Park estate during the making of the Manchester Ship Canal.*

Lyme Hall Cross-head Numbers 1 and 2

The broken remains of Lyme Hall Cross-head Number 1

He explained that they were found nearly fifty years before by "Rough Tom" (Thomas Armfield) when working for Peter Swindells ridding-up gorse bushes on Black Farm, at the north end of Whaley Moor. They were large bushes, and in pulling up the roots, "Tom" found the crosses close together but without any base or foundation to them. Mr Boulton thought that "if they had ever been fixed prominently on the spot we should have had some reference to them handed down by local history; and that, possibly, they had been brought from some other place and buried there, say 200 years ago, or, if they were ever fixed here, how was it there should be two in the same place and so much alike?" The answer may be two ancient boundaries and old road meets near the same place, as in the case of the Fox Lane crosses, Holmesfield-Barlow boundaries and bridle ways meet."

Mr Boulton said:

"the exact place where they were found it is called Badger Clough, or say, the northern end of Long Side, about 100 yards north of the higher end of Red Moor Lane and about 20 yards off the present old road where a very ancient footpath crosses what was formerly the old packhorse road".

This would place the find at (SJ989835) which is approximately 1.6 miles ENE from Lyme Hall.

Badger Clough is not marked on modern maps but is a dry clough which runs behind Longside Cottage and is clearly shown on older maps.

Wherever the cross-heads were found, they were removed for safety to High Lane by the churchwarden, Richard Orford. These cross-heads were once more claimed by the Leghs and set up on separate plinths in the court-yard at Lyme Hall.

Now for the oft repeated statement that these twin cross-heads once stood atop the Bowstones and thus make a complete Mercian Cross. For a start the cross-heads, even when found were not complete, so we cannot claim to have a complete Mercian cross; more's the pity. The central bosses and two arms of both heads were missing when they were found, but from the fragments and those of similar crosses they should have looked similar to the drawing on page 106.

Before proceeding any further it should be reiterated that the section of a Mercian cross above the collar(s) is always roughly square in cross section, while most cross shafts of a rectangular cross section are broader when viewed from the front than the side. This rule cannot be applied universally; Taddington Cross for example has a square cross section. The problem is further complicated by the fact that the various plaits, whorls, and key patterns can appear on both types of crosses. However, on balance it is most likely that the Lyme Hall cross-heads once graced a Mercian twin cross.

When the cross-heads were found accurate sketches were made which show clearly that they were reassembled in an odd way without central bosses. The sketches do show quite clearly that the squared portion below the central bosses was complete. In other words they were broken off immediately above the collar. These cross-heads can be examined at Lyme Hall. Unfortunately one has been broken off recently but by comparing with the drawing of Lyme Hall cross-head No 1, it can be estimated fairly accurately how long it

was. The other has been placed in the Chapel for safety. The dimensions of the cross-heads are as follows:- cross-head No 1, height 28ins with base 9.5ins by 7.5ins; cross-head No 2, height 45.25ins with base 12.5ins by 10.5ins. The complete heads with central bosses would be taller.

Before either of these cross-heads could fit on top of the Bowstones it would be necessary to chisel off the top of the Bowstones shafts level with the collar. Further the Bowstones and the Lyme Hall cross-heads do not appear to be made of the same sandstone. What we need here is the opinion of a skilled stone mason, not some academic poring over ancient documents. I will not believe the cross-heads stood on top of the Bowstones until they are carried down and put in place. To add to the confusion, behind the broken shaft opposite the information office at Lyme Hall is another piece of square cross fragment of a very different coloured stone. Which other Mercian cross did it come from?

Now one thing that needs stating is that stone crosses were once much commoner and the cross heads could have come from yet another twin base or from two Mercian pillar shafts. After the previous finds there is always the distinct possibility that more crosses or fragments might turn up at any minute. Instead of indulging in flights of fancy it would have been better if folks had got hold of a spade and made a search for the missing portions of the cross-heads.

Another possible, but unlikely, explanation is extracted from an article in the *'Athenaeum'* of July 9th, 1904 written by the Rev. J, Charles Cox:

> *"Some two miles from the Bowstones, on Whaley Moor, we also saw a large stone with two squared sockets that at one time had certainly held a pair of crosses, near to a boundary angle and by the side of an old disused road. I have seen a photograph of two Saxon crosses now in Lyme Hall grounds moved there I believe from somewhere in the neighbourhood. Could they have come from this situation?"*

If Rev. Cox said the sockets were square then square they were. The stone the Rev. Cox examined was almost certainly the 'Dipping Stone' located at the southern end of Whaley Moor at (SJ995817). It is just under 1.5 miles from the Bow Stones. I think on this occasion the Rev. Cox was wide of the mark. If the shafts which once stood in the Dipping Stone could be found and they fitted the cross-heads then the suggestion would have considerable merit, but the Lyme Hall cross-heads are of the type normally associated with Mercian Pillar shafts and the holes in the Dipping Stone are undoubtedly rectangular.

To get to the bottom of the reasons for siting some of the crosses around Disley it might be as well to take into consideration the reasons which seem to apply to the majority of other cross sites. It would appear that most crosses stand along old routes and if the same criteria applies to crosses in the Disley area then a different picture emerges.

The old tracks were not the early medieval equivalent of the M1 with horse traffic flowing smoothly in both directions. Rather they were routes picked out by men carrying goods in a pack on their backs or on the backs of one or a small number of horses. Because much of the land had never been farmed, the valley bottoms were often marshy and liable to flooding so these tracks kept to higher drier land where the going was better. When a track became impassable after heavy rain and overuse, the traveller would be compelled to use the bank at the side or one of the many alternative tracks available in open countryside. The foregoing should be borne in mind when considering ancient routes. Modern roads may cover the remains of turnpikes, Roman roads and even older ways, but with the advent of turnpikes, enclosures, more intensive farming leading to the felling of

An impression of an intact Mercian Cross-head

trees and digging of drains and other forms of progress, the old ways would pass from use and can only be detected as holloways and nicks on hill crests. From a high vantage point on the opposite side of a valley it is often possible to make out the lines of old tracks and long demolished buildings which do not appear on any map.

A useful start might be made at the **Dipping Stone,** or **Plague Stone.** (SJ995817) This badly eroded cross base with two rectangular holes which once held the cross shafts is not of the Mercian Pillar type but has been included here for convenience as it may help to explain its own presence and the reasons for the location of other crosses. It closely resembles the twin base in Bolsterstone churchyard. Just why is it in its present location on the south east slope of Whaley Moor? It does not stand on any present boundary, but the boundary between Lyme Handley and Whaley Bridge Civil Parishes is not far away and at one point is heading directly for the Dipping Stone before turning at a right angle to the west.

A closer examination of the Dipping Stone and its situation may provide a few clues. It is obvious that folks have walked round it and climbed all over it which has done nothing for its preservation. It is also noticeable that the stone is not set level in the ground and when it held two heavy upright stone crosses it would have to be set up on a level foundation. The stone is far too heavy to be moved easily, but it could have been rolled over from a position higher on the hillside where it would also have stood out more prominently.

The situation of the Dipping Stone may hold the solution to the siting of a whole list of Crosses. If it is considered as just another wayside cross then it is probably significant that it stands at the northern end of the Macclesfield Forest Ridgeway which came north past Shining Tor, Cats Tor, Pym Chair, Windgather Rocks, Taxal Moor and Whaley Moor, as part of an old route starting in Staffordshire and leading into Yorkshire. There are plenty of paths and old lanes in the vicinity which might be vestiges of this way.

If we travel on northwards from the Dipping Stone we pass close to the spot where the cross-heads now in Lyme Hall were found. (SJ989835). To serve as a way marker these crosses would have been of more value if placed somewhat higher on the moor than where they were found. This could well have been the case, after all crosses were thrown down not up. A search of the moor above the point of discovery might just reveal a few clues. After all, "Rough Tom" found the crosses close together but without any base or foundation to them. The missing central bosses and arms should be buried nearby and the shafts, base or bases ought not to be too far away either. A useful start might be made by walking over this part of Whaley Moor and considering where one would place a prominent way marker from the point of view of a traveller when there were no modern roads. Disley Church should also be visible from this site as the next cross along the route.

Nearby Redmoor Lane leads directly to New Mills and once across the River Goyt it is not far to Pole Lane via Castle Edge Road. Here at last we may have the reason for the remarkable line of crosses which once lined the route from Arnfield Pole to the Picking Rods. Once again they were way markers.

The route following the old Roman road from Buxton to Whaley Bridge had four known crosses and after crossing the Goyt at Whaley Bridge it could continue past the Dipping Stone, then head for Disley Church and on towards Stockport and Manchester. This theory could account for the siting of the Dipping Stone but leaves us no wiser as to why a double cross was erected in the first place. At least it does not leave the Picking Rods as the sole example of a twin cross way marker on a piece of open moor. If the twin cross-heads now at Lyme Hall were once part of twin crosses standing above Badger Clough then we have the unique example of three twin crosses in sequence.

The names Dipping Stone and Plague Stone recall stories of the Eyam plague and how money was left in exchange for food at the Boundary Stone which has holes cut into it so that coins could be dipped in vinegar. The story of the Eyam plague is well known but many other communities were visited by bubonic plague between the Black Death and 1665. Incidentally the Eyam Boundary Stone is rounded like many others. Was it yet another glacial boulder cleared from a field and used as a boundary marker?

Below: The Dipping Stone on Whaley Moor

8 MISCELLANEOUS CROSSES

This is a section devoted to crosses and similar antiquities which do not always fit easily into one of the foregoing sections. Some of the crosses mentioned no longer exist other than as names on a map, but taking into consideration the way in which other lost crosses have turned up, they are worthy of mention as a guide to further searches.

There is no shortage of place names including the word cross which usually indicates a former cross site, many of these might repay a closer study. Near Monyash is the Mycross Mine and a Cross Lane; there are other Cross Lanes near Dethick and Hoylandswaine, and a Crosslow at SK162555. There are several Cross Farms such as the one near Crich at SK348546, and at SK146668 near Monyash. There is a Cross Flat Plantation at SK193638. These names should be treated with some caution, every Cross Street in the middle of a town is not an indication of a former cross site, it may just be a way of crossing from one street to another. There is no guarantee that a cross once stood at Cross Gates (SK085633). "Gate" is the Norse equivalent to the Saxon "Way" and in this instance it certainly indicates a point where two packhorse ways intersected.

Bakewell Market Hall

References to a cross fragment in the Old Market Hall appear from time to time in various books and articles. This was on loan to the Information Centre from Bakewell Church and it has now been returned to the south porch of the church.

Birchover

A crucifixion has been crudely carved into the wall of a small cave known as the Hermit's Cave, or the Cratcliffe Hermitage near Robin Hood's Stride. It has a small niche for a lamp or candle and may date from around 1300 AD. According to Tom Bates in 'Discovering Derbyshire's White Peak', hermits were appointed by bishops to safeguard and offer hospitality to travellers. The cave is quite close to the section of the old Portway between Winster and Alport. The carving has been spoiled by vandals in the past and is now made relatively secure with stout iron railings. There is a well established yew tree outside the cave which is most likely older than the carving and suggests that this is a piece of ancient woodland which has never seen the woodman's axe. Saints and hermits lived in caves in various other parts of England. Saint Cuthbert in the Eden Valley at Wetheral in Cumbria is another example.

Birgwurd Cross

From 'Memorials of Old Derbyshire' by Rev. Cox we obtain the following intriguing piece of information:

"There are two other sites in the Peak District marked on these early plans of 1640 where a pair of stones, each surmounted by a cross, is figured, neither of which has been identified. One of these is also on the northern edge of the Mellor Commons, the Birgwurd Cross, the outline of which is here given."

Now if we assume that Rev. Cox is correct and the Birgwurd cross was on the northern edge of the Mellor Commons and twin crosses were located where three or more boundaries met, then the most likely site would have been on Coombes Rocks at SK017915, where the Townships of Charlesworth, Chisworth, Simmondley and Thornsett meet.

A cross standing on Coombes Rocks would have been quite a landmark clearly visible from many directions. The edge will have receded in the intervening years, and the cross could have been thrown down over the edge, but a search of the site on the edge and among the fallen stones below revealed no trace of cross or base.

There may be no trace of a cross on Cown Edge, but another antiquity in the shape of the ancient dyke which marks the boundary between Simmondley and Thornsett can be found running parallel with the wall between SK017915 and 018915.

Here the matter of the Birgwurd Cross must rest for the moment until more information on the reasons for constructing twin crosses is unearthed. The Rev. Cox mentions two sites for twin crosses in the Peak District. This does not restrict the search to Derbyshire; the Dipping Stone or the Disley Church sites might just provide the answer.

Cown Edge

In a disused quarry on Cown Edge Rocks above Rocks Farm at approximately (SK019916) in recent times someone went to the trouble of producing a religious carving. Originally it was a crucifixion, but it has been so despoiled by stone throwers as to be unrecognisable.

Crossgate

In Tintwistle at (SK018976) is a property called Crossgate situated on Crossgate Lane. One would expect that the cross stood a little to the north east of this house beside the road from Tintwistle to the hamlet of Arnfield and heading for Mossley although no obvious trace remains.

Derwent Cross

In the Transactions of the Hunter Archaeological Society for 1991 there is a report of the remains of a cross shaft spotted among the ruins of Derwent village in the autumn of 1990 when the very low rainfall that year caused the water level to fall sufficiently. It could be seen that the stone had been carved but it was not possible to examine it more closely until the water level fell again in the autumn of the following year. Unfortunately during the intervening period, the stone had been damaged by stone throwing vandals and about 8ins broken off and the carvings on one face obliterated. The remnant is just under 2ft in length and has one face carved with circles and interlacing. It appears to be of the same pattern as other crosses in the area. There could be a connection with this portion of a cross shaft and the cross base built into the Derwent packhorse bridge now at Slippery Stones. Presumably this cross base was used as building materials when the bridge was rebuilt around 1672 by Henry Balguy at the same time as he built Derwent Hall.

The main thrust of the article is to demonstrate the likelihood of there having been a religious building on the site in medieval times. This seems a likely scenario, but the reason for mentioning this broken cross shaft here is to show that finds can crop up throughout the area.

Elton Moor Crosshead

Among his many finds, Thomas Bateman lists part of a Saxon Cross dug up on Elton Moor in 1842. Unfortunately he does not give a more accurate description of the site so it is impossible to allot it to some old route. The fragment consists of the boss and one arm of the cross with triquetra and appears to have been of the type associated with round shafted crosses. It is probably to be found among the other pieces in Bakewell Church.

Crosshead found on Elton Moor

High Cross

Nothing remains today at SK136602, but the name lives on as a name on the map near Hartington on the route of the packhorse way to Middleton-by-Youlgreave via Heathcote.

Hollincross Lane

Robert Hamnett, the Glossop historian, writing at the end of the nineteenth century, mentions the Hollin Cross as one of the lost crosses around Glossop. There was no sign of a cross in his day and he would certainly have made it his business to enquire of old inhabitants. Hollincross Lane once extended part way up Freetown and the medieval track between the hamlets of Whitfield and Simmondley would pass this way. From the preamble to the Act for the building of the Chapel-en-le-Frith to Entreclough Turnpike road it is clear that there was a road in existence in a ruinous condition, before 1790, which would cross the former track near to where St James' church stands today. The Hollin Cross probably stood close to the present crossroads at SK032936.

Hope Guide Stoop

(SK161874) Guide stoops were set up in response to Acts of Parliament at the end of the eighteenth century along packhorse ways and some have gained the name of cross. Hope Cross and Moscar Cross are typical examples, but there are plenty of others. One obvious explanation in some cases is that they stand at a cross roads. It is abundantly clear that the majority of ancient crosses stood at significant points along old routes so it is hardly surprising that when guide stoops were set up that they should be sited at or close to the same spots.

Hope Cross stands around 7ft high with a capstone bearing the names of Sheffield, Glossop, Edale and Hope on its faces. It also has the date 1737 cut into the top of the shaft which is probably the date when it was restored. The packhorse ways between the places indicated crossed at the spot and this could be a good enough reason for the cross name, however, these routes are ancient and there could well have been a cross there previously. The boundary between Hope and Derwent Civil Parishes also passes by this guide stoop. Anyone interested in learning more about local guide stoops should read the excellent books on the subject written by Howard Smith.

Hope Guide Stoop

Jenkin Cross

(SJ983765) Jenkin Chapel is believed to stand on the site of Jenkin Cross. Jenkin Chapel stands along the route of the saltway from Middlewich through Macclesfield, Buxton, Tideswell, and the Curbar Gap to Chesterfield. These saltways were in use long before the Norman Conquest and Fox Hill to the west of Jenkin Chapel would seem an ideal spot for a cross intended as a way marker.

Monyash

Fragments of a cross were found near One Ash Grange Farm during the course of archaeological fieldwork by the Department of Prehistory and Archaeology of the University of Sheffield. The actual finds were at SK16396458 on the surface of a rubble-filled

Cross arms from Monyash set up
in Buxton Museum

mining hollow. The pieces of cross arm are now in Buxton Museum, mounted on a papier mache shaft. The remnants of two cross arms were found; one had bosses which had been chiselled into shape, but the other had no trace of a boss so they came from different cross heads. In Buxton Museum there was already a cross arm of similar form with bosses which appear to have been part of a wheel head cross. All three pieces are remarkably similar to the arms on the cross-heads at Lyme Hall. Could it be that the piece already in Buxton Museum came from one of the crosses along the route of the Roman Road? the Woman's Cross or Wainstones Cross for example?

Moor Lodge

SK022854 This pillar and base stand in the front garden of Moor Lodge on Over Hill Road which may be an old track, and at a meeting point of footpaths. It does not coincide with any modern boundary. There is something not quite right about this shaft; if it is indeed a cross shaft. The shaft which is basically of a square section without any taper is unlike any other I have seen and the top has been cut square as if intended for a sundial. There is no trace of interlaced carving. The base in which it is set looks suspiciously like a millstone and this is mounted upon a circular stone wall which is provided with a couple of steps. It reminds one of the sundial near Mottram church which was erected in 1760 and looks of a similar age. If it once bore a sundial then the steps would have been necessary to climb high enough to see it. Anyone with arthritic knees would have been glad of it in mounting a horse. I am left wondering with this stone pillar. It is unlikely that if someone had erected it in their garden as a sundial they would have made it so high. Was it moved to its present position by someone who just fancied the look of it as an ornament to their property? A nice thing to have in one's garden, but I am very doubtful if it ever was part of a cross.

Stone Column at Moor Lodge

Prestbury Cross

The Saxon Cross in the churchyard at Prestbury is rather unusual partly due to the way the three parts have been reassembled. The bottom two fit well enough together but the top piece gives the impression that there is something missing, or that it comes from another cross. The mutilated fragments making up this cross were found embedded in the walls of the church. Perhaps some of the missing parts will turn up some day buried in the churchyard and give us a better idea of what this cross once looked like.

Richard's Cross

Suggested by some to have been a boundary marker on the borders of the possessions of Richard de Lovetot. A quoin stone which can be seen in the south-east corner of an outbuilding at The Oaks Farm, (SK239994), near Midhope, may be part of the remains of such a cross.

Roe Cross

(SJ985966) There is no sign of a cross at this point today, but there is the well known White Stone which stands beside the old track which was in existence long before Mottram Cutting was driven through the saddle between Harrop Edge and Shaw Moor. The suggestion has been made that the name comes from Roads Cross, but the White Stone would have been suitably situated for a cross base or as a marker stone visible to travellers coming from several directions. The boundaries of Hollingworth, Mottram and Matley are somewhat convoluted but appear to meet very close to the White Stone.

White Stone above Mottram Cutting

Rushton Spencer

A cross site is marked at (SJ933621) close to a footpath and not far distant from the Staffordshire Way.

Sheffield Museum

Here is a cast of a cross shaft complete with vine scrolls, bunches of grapes and the figure of an archer crouched at the base, shooting at some creature concealed in the foliage at the top. The original shaft of this cross is now housed in the British Museum. It was discovered in a cutler's workshop with one side hollowed out to make a quenching trough.

There are differing views as to its provenance; one suggestion is that it may have been the "Great Cross in the churchyard at Sheffield," which was demolished in 1570; another is that it was brought from Derbyshire. It certainly has many features in common with the crosses at Bakewell and Bradbourne.

Simmondley Cross

In Bulmer's *'Derbyshire'* on the list of residents for Simmondley in 1895 appear James Bennett of Simmondley and Cross Farm, and John Bowden, of White Cross. The 1891 Census is of some help giving James Bennett, aged 69, of 81 Simmondley Lane, Farmer, and John Bowden, aged 55, at 69 Simmondley Lane, Machine Calico printer. As you approach

Cross shaft cast in Weston Park
Museum, Sheffield

Simmondley village from the direction of Dinting, the odd numbers are on the left hand side, and the 1899 six inches to the mile scale map shows only two properties which were located just on the bend below Simmondley Hall. The Victorian Ordnance Survey Map shows no properties at the Dinting end of the lane.

Burdett's Map shows a track from Higher Dinting to Simmondley which took a somewhat different route to the modern road, but which would have aligned with the stretch where these two properties stood. I would estimate that the White Cross stood at SK021934.

Windyway Cross

SK058490 The present standing stone is dated 1882 and is a replacement of an earlier way marker which probably long before that time replaced a wayside cross. From 1770, the packhorse way from the Duke of Devonshire's copper mines at Ecton passed this point *en route* to the smelting works at Whiston. It would be visible on the ridge for some distance for south bound traffic.

Ousley Cross

At Ousley Cross Farm at SK125446 about a mile south of Stanton to the west of Ashbourne (see p.126).

Harley Cross Gate

The cross is marked at SK077688 on an old packhorse track between Brierlow Bar and Flash. There is a Stoop Farm at SK063682 a mile further along the same track.

This list of crosses will continue to grow with every old map or document examined and the further we travel from the Peak. There is Thompson Cross in Stalybridge and Hurst Cross near Ashton-under Lyne, and where for example was the site of the Gee Cross near Hyde?

EPILOGUE

Having strolled across village greens, rambled along country lanes and tramped resolutely over desolate windswept moors it is now time to try and draw some conclusions about the crosses we have discovered. Why were the crosses erected in the first place and why were they placed in their particular sites? If we could answer this question satisfactorily we would have a very good idea of where to look to find some of the missing crosses of the region.

The answer in the case of memorial crosses is self evident. Market crosses also do not pose a problem since they were erected in some convenient central position when villages and small towns had reached a size where a market was required. Typical local examples are Castleton 1222; Bakewell 1254; Ashbourne 1257; Alstonfield 1308.

Thus we are left with churchyard crosses and the vast majority of the remainder which can best be described as wayside crosses. It seems most likely that crosses were set up on previously pagan sites as part of the process of the conversion of England to Christianity and that some few were left standing when churches were built on the site. Many of these must have been thrown down in the time of Edward VI which would explain how some have been discovered by sextons years later and resurrected, such as the one which presently stands in Ecclesfield Church. Others would be redundant when a stone church was erected in Norman times and be utilised as building material. There are countless examples of carved stones incorporated in churches and of others being found during renovations.

Now for the altogether more contentious subject of wayside crosses.

Writing in *Memorials of Old Derbyshire*, the Rev Charles Cox has the following to say:

"*In a paper contributed to the Reliquary many years ago, when under the editorship of historian Mr. Llewellynn Jewitt, it was asserted with some confidence that these crosses marked out the three great divisions or wards of the Forest of Peak. This was a natural kind of guess to make, but investigation immediately proved that such a supposition was quite baseless. With the possible solitary exception of the cross on the old pack-horse track from the head of Edale into Hayfield, not one of these crosses has any possible connection with forest bounds. Nor are they, as has been conjectured by another writer, terminal stones of monastic lands, for we know with a fair amount of accuracy the directions in which such lands lay, and in no case do these crosses correspond with such limits. It is also quite obvious that for the most part these Peak crosses cannot, by any stretch of imagination, be described as mere wayside crosses, either to mark some special incident or tragedy, or to excite the Christian devotion of the wayfarer; and this for the simple reason that the majority of the crosses do not appear to have been on any frequented track of either the remote or nearer past. Nor is it possible to conceive, by those who have visited any number of them, that they could have been utilised for the purposes of guiding or general direction.*

It is, of course, far easier to say what they were not, than to arrive at any true solution as to what was their general object or design. The solution that so far seems the most probable has already been elsewhere succinctly stated without awakening adverse criticism. All those crosses that have been hitherto identified by myself and friends during three rambles with the old plans in our hands in three successive years, have been on important boundary lines. I believe almost the whole of them are pre-Norman, and I am at present strongly inclined to believe that they mark the setting out of ecclesiastical divisions or parishes, or parochial chapelries, soon after the reconversion of England had become an established fact, and when Christianity, under the ordering of Theodore and Wilfred, was becoming definitely organised and ceasing to be mere scattered groups of missionary stations......It is obvious that if ecclesiastical bounds were to be marked out in a comparatively wild and treeless district, something artificial would be needed in far greater abundance than in ordinary districts, where large trees, river banks, ancient roads or lands pertaining to particular holders, could readily be named and utilised for boundary purposes.

The supposition that these crosses are of a township or parish boundary character is much strengthened by the frequency of their occurrence in the exact places where there are proofs of fairly early cultivation, and where there were rather intricate intersections of such divisions."

Now the Rev. Charles Cox was an astute observer and he is certainly correct when he points out that many of the crosses are sited along township boundaries, but I must take issue with him when he says that:

"that the majority of the crosses do not appear to have been on any frequented track of either the remote or nearer past. Nor is it possible to conceive, by those who have visited any number of them, that they could have been utilised for the purposes of guiding or general direction."

Catshaw, Charlesworth, Clulow, Edale, Hollins, and Martinside crosses to pick just a few from the dozens of examples, are certainly located on old tracks and placed so as to be clearly visible to travellers approaching from either direction. Indeed so carefully were they placed that it is possible to find where they stood when only the base remains

hidden among the roadside herbage by studying the slope of the track on either side. The Rev. Cox refers to three rambles in search of ancient crosses, but I would contend that more accurate conclusions can be drawn from an inspection of the sites of over a hundred wayside crosses distributed through the region.

The statement that many crosses stand on parish boundaries is indisputable but parish boundaries were set along streams and rivers, along ancient tracks which in some cases were Roman roads; prominent stones and tors, long lived oaks and hawthorns were all pressed into service. The question that gets right to the nub of the matter is: are there any crosses marking a boundary that are not also on an old route? The answer to the best of my knowledge is none. From a total of 103 wayside crosses discovered so far, 31 definitely stand on boundaries and alongside routes, but 72 more stand on ancient ways and are not serving as boundary markers. Ergo, the notion that crosses were set up as boundary markers is erroneous. I would suggest that many of these crosses were set up before parish boundaries were fixed and that they were used later as convenient markers already in place.

It may be significant that the Rev. Cox visited the Mellor-Thornsett area, where so many crosses do stand along a boundary, before writing the above. In fact in an article entitled *'Early Crosses in the High Peak'*, which appeared in the *'Athenaeum'* dated July 9th 1904, he states with reference to the suggestion that the crosses marked the Bounds of the Forest of Peak:

"I had various reasons for doubting this statement and a careful examination of the extant maps, drawn by the commissioners in 1638-40, of the commons and wastes within the Forest, at the time when the project of disafforesting was intended to be carried out, convinced me to the contrary."

These maps were concerned with the setting out of boundaries, so it is hardly surprising that he came to such a conclusion. I must also confess that for some time until the evidence became overwhelming, I tended to agree with him.

The Rev. Cox also doubts whether crosses were used to mark the bounds of monastic lands. He mighty be right in thinking they were not set up for that purpose, but there are crosses mentioned in charters concerned with grants of land. I suspect that the crosses were in place before the land grants were made and served as useful permanent marks. His other statement that crosses were set in the exact places where there are proofs of fairly early cultivation will not stand up to a close examination in many cases.

The subject of parish boundaries is made more complex by the divisions that have taken place with the increase in population and building of new churches. The ancient Parish of Glossop contained nineteen townships stretching from Padfield in the north to Bugsworth and Brownside in the south. (Map 7) The townships are almost certainly based on the manors in each area which might well go back to Roman times or even earlier. Domesday carefully records each manor as a unit for taxing. A study of the map of this ancient parish showing the townships and the sites of the known cross sites shows only one, Edale Cross, on the parish boundary. There are four crosses along the boundary of the Manor of Glossop, all of which also lie on old ways.

In a line south of the Picking Rods are four crosses on the boundary between Mellor and Thornsett which may lead to the Dipping Stone, and a further cross on the boundary between Mellor and Whitle. It may be pure coincidence, but Mellor is the only township lying outside the Manor of Glossop which was not in the district known as Bowden Middlecale. This poses yet another as yet unanswered question; why should this division require a line of crosses placed so closely together? The cross on the boundary between Charlesworth and Simmondley stood beside Monks Road and

the remaining crosses are all wayside crosses with no apparent connection with boundaries of any description. There is no clear link between the parish church in Glossop and the chapels at Hayfield and Mellor as far as crosses along the way are concerned.

It is quite clear that the vast majority of crosses are set along ancient ways and as they are so often set in positions chosen so that the next cross along the route can be seen, to call them way markers is perfectly sensible. However, it still leaves questions unanswered. Who erected them? Why were they erected? Were they set up along all old routes? When were they erected?

The first question is very difficult to deal with. The early missionaries would preach in the open air and when churches were built they would be of wood so that no trace remains. To erect crosses in stone would require the services of skilled masons who would want paying. Perhaps local Saxon landowners were prepared to pay in addition to giving land to the Church. Later, with the building of monasteries, the wealth would become available and the need for guidance between religious establishments a sensible provision, as well as constantly reminding travellers of the Christian message. An elaborately carved cross such as the one in Eyam churchyard must have taken a mason weeks to carve, but many crosses seem to have been plain, if the surviving stumps are any guide. Carved crosses do appear at, or close to, old churches such as Bakewell and Bradbourne and there are plenty of plain crosses on desolate moors. There does seem to be some correlation between carved crosses and old churches but Beeley Cross and the cross which once stood on Eccles Pike are ornately carved and stood on open moor beside old ways.

As to why they were erected other than reminders of religion, much of the country was still open heath and moorland and to be able to follow a line of clear landmarks must have been invaluable. For the benefit of those who have never tramped across rough open moorland it might be as well to explain the value of landmarks. It is often quite

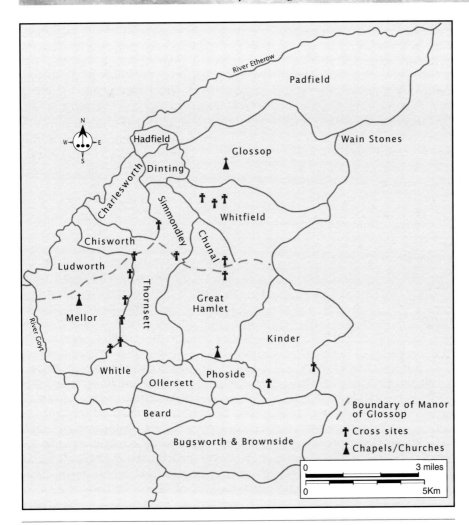

Map 7: Distribution of Crosses in the Ancient Parish of Glossop

impossible to walk in a straight line towards one's objective because of obstacles such as boggy ground, thick bracken hiding broken ground, or ravines. The solution to the problem is to pick out a landmark at some distance along your intended course and head for it by the easiest route avoiding as many obstacles as possible and after negotiating each one, head once more for your landmark. In time the easiest route would be found. Here we see the value of standing stones, lone trees, peculiar shaped rocks, and of course crosses.

While nearly all the evidence points to crosses being set up as way markers it does not fully explain why the early church in England should go to the trouble and expense of erecting ornate crosses, and especially twin crosses on open moorland when a crude standing stone would have served the same purpose. There must have been considerable motivation to account for the erection of hundreds of crosses in an age when most folks lived in huts and even ealdormen lived in wooden halls. One is reminded of the huge investment in cathedral building a few hundred years later.

The Anglo-Saxons had until recently been pagan peoples and in a superstitious age would cling to beliefs in their ancient gods and practices which the Roman Church would want to stamp out or convert to their own use. Crosses would certainly remind travellers that they were in a country claimed for Christianity and carvings could illustrate the Christian message with scenes such as the crucifixion.

That crosses were set up along old routes is incontrovertible, but were they set up along all routes, or only on selected ones. Certain ways between outlying villages and the parish church were known as "Coffin Roads," "Corpse Roads," or "Burying Roads". The dead had to be buried in consecrated ground which meant carrying the coffins to the parish church and crosses were set up along the route where the coffins could be put down for a while and prayers could be said for the dead. Hollins Cross at the top of the hill between Edale and Hope provides a good example and it is not difficult to imagine the pall bearers being glad of the rest after climbing such a steep way. These coffin roads are not restricted to the Peak and examples can be found all over England, their former existence being revealed by such names as "Berrying Lane" or even "Church Lane."

One possible explanation for the siting of wayside crosses is that they were placed along routes between old religious establishments and it would be possible to draw up a list of crosses which do in fact lie along such ways. Churches could be controlled from a distant monastery, such as Glossop from Basingwerke in North Wales, and clergy and their servants would need to travel frequently between their various possessions.

The theory that crosses were set up on routes linking old churches has its attractions, but such churches would be built in the larger villages which would be the very places that most people would be travelling between. Even the early wooden churches would be much larger than peasant dwellings and a mark for travellers to aim for. Before the Dispossession, monasteries provided food and lodging for travellers who would be glad of route markers in strange open country. Villagers would know the route to their parish church well enough, but pedlars, packmen and all travellers who were strangers would

need some guidance. The crosses might also have been set up in such a manner as to give an indication of the direction of the next cross along the way. The Rev. Cox mentions a groove cut into the base of Martinside Cross which could have served this purpose and the New Cross near Penistone also has a groove cut in its base. The problem with interpreting the reasoning behind such marks is that bases have often been moved in the intervening centuries.

One thing which should be borne in mind is that in Anglo-Saxon times, churches were few and far between and the population small. In Derbyshire, Ashbourne, Ashover, Bakewell, Bradbourne, Hope and Darley Abbey, are all mentioned in the Domesday Survey. In Staffordshire, the first Cathedral at Lichfield may have been built as early as 700 AD. There were monasteries at Dieulacres (Leek), Croxden and Calwich. Alstonfield, Cheddleton, Ilam and Leek had churches. In Cheshire, Stockport, Macclesfield, and Mottram were all established in the twelfth century and probably far earlier. Bishops could hold manors in various counties, often at a considerable distance and route markers would have been invaluable. The fact that a church is not mentioned in Domesday does not mean that one did not exist. In 1086, many must have been burned down in the "Harrying of the North" and not rebuilt until years afterwards.

With few churches so widely spaced it is obvious that the bulk of the population could never visit a church regularly and clergy would need to travel to preach to them. Indeed the number of churches in Derbyshire was still inadequate up to the middle of the nineteenth century and it is not unknown to find a whole family baptised on the same day. With such large parishes the vicar would have to wait until some farmer could be persuaded to bring his family to the church from an outlying district.

If the crosses were erected prior to the Norman Conquest and were also intended to mark the routes between religious establishments then there must have been churches in existence before they actually appear in records. The name Ecclesfield suggests the existence of a church in late Roman times. The huge ancient parish of Bradfield with its many cross sites might be a good place to start an investigation into the siting of crosses. Other old churches in the area would be Sheffield, Bolsterstone, and Penistone. We know the names of many of these crosses even if nothing remains and it is possible to make a reasonable guesstimate of where a few of them stood if we assume that they followed the line of the road from Bradfield church to say Sheffield and were placed so as to be within sight of each other. Ones Moor Cross should have been at approximately (SK281922) on the appropriately named Kirk Edge Road; Rotherham Cross at (SK290921); and Worral Cross in the village of that name a little further on. There should be more cross sites between Worral and Sheffield, but they will have disappeared under bricks and mortar.

Within the parish of Bradfield there are other possible routes. Starting from Bradfield Church there are cross sites at Swan Height, White Lea, then a gap brought about by Broomhead and More Hall Reservoirs before we come to Bolsterstone Church. Beyond Bolsterstone Church there is a house called Cross on Stone Moor Road at SK26449738; a Cross Lane at SK25459878 (now a built up area), and another Cross Lane at SE260014 and finally Penistone Church. Along the way from Midhope to Bradfield are Uden (Ewden Height) Cross, Kennards Cross (Canyards), and Handsome Cross.

Abbey Grange Farm at the bottom of Abbey Clough in the Upper Derwent Valley was an appendage of the Abbey of Welbeck and if we follow the route up Abbey Clough and head for Bradfield along Emlin Dike Road, we pass a Cross Hill and then the New Cross on the tops before dropping down into Bradfield Dale where there was a Romescar Cross on Cross Lane and then the cross at the Cross Inn in Low Bradfield (which is now in Bradfield Church) before turning towards the church. Starting from Ecclesfield Church and heading for Bradfield we pass a Cross House and after passing through Grenoside we come to the Birley Stone on the strangely named Whalejaw or Jaw Bone Hill. There should be other crosses near Oughtibridge and between Oughtibridge and Kirk Edge Road, before finally arriving at Bradfield Church.

There are clearly gaps along the routes listed, which is hardly surprising after the lapse of 1,000 years. Some of these gaps might be filled from a study of tithe maps which usually give the names of the fields and old tracks now hidden under tarmac or flooded beneath the waters of some nineteenth century reservoir. Cross bases can turn up when roads are being widened, or when a ditch is being cleared, or as we have seen, in use as an ornament in someone's garden, the owner blissfully unaware of its provenance.

Are there routes without crosses? One route which is certainly ancient is the track from the Upper Derwent Valley to Penistone known as Cut Gate and formerly as Cart Gate which name gives some indication of its former importance. I know of no crosses along this route between the packhorse bridge which stood in Derwent Village and Hartcliffe Cross, a distance of eight miles as the crow flies and probably nearer to ten on the ground and much of it rugged going. There may have been no crosses along this route, but there were certainly way markers. In the days when flocks of sheep were driven from the Derwent Valley over to Penistone, Halifax, and other Yorkshire towns, there were two possible routes for part of the way. One followed the valley north as far as Slippery Stones before heading north-east up Cranberry Clough and then zig-zagged up the steep climb to the top of Cut Gate. This route had the advantage of being more sheltered for much of the way and would be more suitable for those starting from higher in the valley. The alternative route turned off further south up Howden Clough and passed between two upright standing stones at SK181942, known as Penistone Stile and then headed for two wooden posts which stood near the summit of Cut Gate. These wooden posts were still standing in 1914 but have long since rotted away. The stones which comprised Penistone Stile were still standing around 1985, but have disappeared from the site and with truly remarkable promptitude also from the latest maps.

Another old track which predates the Romans is the one from Ashbourne to Buxton over the well drained limestone. I know of no cross along the whole length of this route unless the base now in Tissington churchyard once stood beside it.

The next problem to be addressed is that of twin crosses set in a single base. It has been suggested that these were set up where three or more parish boundaries meet. This is much more difficult to assess because there are so few of them. Of the seven possible crosses so far discovered in this category, the site of the Birgwurd Cross is a matter for conjecture and so can add nothing of value. The Picking Rods stand at the junction of four township boundaries and are probably the reason for the idea being mooted in the first place, and if the stone at present in Bolsterstone churchyard came originally from Unsliven Bridge, then we have a second example. This leaves us with Ecclesfield, Bolsterstone, Disley and possibly Penistone churches where twin bases have been discovered which at least suggests that twin crosses are more likely to be connected in some way with old churches. The last example, the Dipping Stone is of little or no value in trying to solve the problem. There are boundaries heading towards it which suddenly turn away, but this is not so striking as to seem significant. The Bowstones also have boundaries heading for them which suddenly turn aside, but as we have seen, the Bowstones no longer stand in their original position.

The Dipping Stone on Whaley Moor and the Picking Rods may have stood along old tracks, but what was so important about these sites that it was thought necessary to invest all the labour required in carving and erecting such large stone monuments?

Are there any single shafted crosses standing where three or more boundaries meet? The first point to make is that very few crosses actually stand where boundaries meet. Arnfield Pole stands at the junction of Mellor, Whitle and Thornsett townships; Moscar Cross stood at the junction of Bradfield, Bamford and Derwent; and Pym Chair where

Kettleshulme, Rainow and Whaley Bridge meet. Robin Hood's Cross as we have seen is another example. Among other possible examples are Poyntoncross Barn, Fulshaw Cross and the Lady's Cross, but in the case of the first two we do not know exactly where they stood and the Lady's Cross may not ever have stood on a boundary.

There is no guarantee that the present parish boundary is the same as that laid down possibly 1,000 years ago before the Norman Conquest. Indeed there have been instances of arguments which have even degenerated into violence over exactly where the boundaries lay, and there are records of the questioning of old inhabitants in an effort to decide where they lay when it came to apportioning land for enclosure.

Another suggestion for the existence of twin crosses is that they also occur in north Africa and that when the Moslems advanced across the region and into southern Spain, many Christians were driven out and travelled into Europe bringing their skills with them. Certainly the time frame is right for this to have occurred.

After studying twin shafted crosses in the region, the only conclusion that can be drawn from the information available at present is that insufficient is known to come to a decision as to the reason for their making or siting.

When were the crosses erected? This is perhaps the hardest question of all to answer, but it is likely that the some churchyard crosses were the forerunners of the church and were later incorporated in the structure and that wayside crosses were already in existence when the parishes were set out in the century before the Norman Conquest. It would seem that the Danish part of the population was quickly converted to Christianity with the re-conquest of the Danelaw and that the Roman Catholic Church became an important arm of the Anglo-Saxon state because it possessed the educated monks capable of preparing deeds to Manors, monasteries and other property.

England must have been made up of different tribal groups at this time and it has been suggested that this accounts for the differing styles of cross and ornamentation. It is certainly true that crosses can be grouped into types such as the Mercian pillar crosses or those with rectangular shafts at Bakewell or Sheffield, but the areas where they can be found overlap to a considerable degree and occasionally designs that are considered typical for an area appear miles away.

Derbyshire was under Danish rule for a considerable time, but at a distance from the county town there are few examples of Danish place names which strongly suggests that the original population continued living much as before, but with new overlords. The Pecsaetna may well have consisted largely of remnants of the former Celtic population under Anglian or Danish overlords. Styles of crosses might be connected with the survival of groups such as Celts, Danes or Norse-Irish Vikings establishing the extent of their territory. All perfectly reasonable explanations, but it should not be forgotten that the period was not called the Dark Ages for nothing. Much has been written about pagan symbols appearing on crosses as examples of Norse influence, but all the Germanic groups had similar pagan beliefs before being converted to Christianity. The Angles before coming to Britain had occupied an area immediately to the south of Denmark and may well have thought of themselves as having more in common with the Danish invaders than their Saxon neighbours to the south.

With most of the cross sites, all that remains is a stump and base, or the base only. The majority of these bases have a rectangular mortice which should rule out the possibility of their once supporting Mercian type pillar crosses. This leads to an odd state of affairs. The only cross-heads clearly from rectangular shafted crosses are at Eyam and at Wheston plus some fragments in Bakewell Church and elsewhere, and yet there seem to be more cross-head fragments from Mercian style cross shafts. After examining the remaining rectangular cross shafts it would appear that they can be divided almost equally into those with a plain shaft and those with ornate carving. If those with plain shafts had plain cross heads then fragments used as building material would

hardly be noticed which might explain why they have not been recognised.

It has been pointed out that several of the crosses or bases have marks cut into them apart from the efforts of vandals. These marks generally take the form of capital letters, usually letters only involving cutting straight lines. These marks were put there as part of surveys in relatively recent times. They certainly have nothing to do with the erection of crosses. All the crosses listed can be classified as boundary crosses. The marks can be listed as follows:-

Bow Stones H.L. N.
Pym Chair PC
Hollingworth Head NRT
Lady's Cross T. and I.R. 1618
Picking Rods N
Shuckstone Cross AELW
Shallcross H.L. 1720

How many wayside crosses were there in medieval times? At best I would estimate that we may have examined a fifth of them in the region. True there are lengths of ancient trackways where several crosses can be identified within sight of each other but there are far more where this does not apply.

In addition to crosses being used as boundary and way markers there are plenty of standing stones which serve the same purpose. Interestingly enough there is one in a former lay-by at SK134998. It has a bench mark cut into it, but somehow I cannot imagine that anyone would deliberately set up such a large rock for this purpose. It also lies on the route of the first turnpike road to Saltersbrook which presumably followed the same general line as that used by the jaggers before the route was turnpiked. The top edge of this stone is roughly chisel shaped and this edge is aligned with the Lady Cross.

We shall never discover the exact locations of most of the missing crosses, but fascinating glimpses appear in old records. For example when the commissioners, set the task of deciding the boundaries of Bowden Chapel with the parishes of Hope and Glossop, were gathering evidence on 6th January 1640 at the house of the widow Jane Mosley in Shallcross, many of those questioned were in their eighties and could remember walking the bounds in procession. They described the bounds of Chapel with parts of Wormhill constabulary lying in Hope parish as follows:

"From the end of the old Whaley bridge to a cross called Cross Cliff or Cross in the Broom or Broomfield, thence to Rowting Clough, over the Brown Edge to the long edge 'as the water falls to Wainstones Cross'; then to the Archer's Walls and over the Moss to Derwins Lowe to a stone called the Hanging Stone, and so to Doveholes Kiln."

Now many of these features can still be picked out but they do not coincide at all points with the modern boundary. The Hanging Rock seems well off the route and as to the whereabouts of the Cross in the Broom? I could not even hazard a guess, unless gorse be substituted for broom. Yet it must have been well known to the old folks of the day.

The best way to uncover these old boundary markers is to start by consulting the oldest maps you can lay your hands on and try to relate items found to their map reference on a modern map of at least 2.5 inches to the mile scale. It is possible to make a fair estimate of where the best points are for crosses to be set up within sight of each other, but in the end nothing can compare with putting on a pair of stout boots and walking along old tracks to examine the lay of the land first hand.

There seems to be a policy in the region of neglecting minor roads so that many of them are becoming unsuitable for vehicular traffic and already several resemble medieval tracks. I have not come across any footpads or highwaymen yet, but that is surely only a matter of time. This neglect of road repair may pose considerable inconvenience to the motorist but it is creating some delightful walks. You may not find a cross in your travels, but at any turn in the road there is sure to be something of interest. A sparrow hawk suddenly swooping over the hedge, a

profusion of bluebells on a shady bank, a thin bright-eyed pencil of life darting across the road as a weasel heads for cover, an old bridge which once was an important link on the main thoroughfare and is now covered in lichen, the remains of a leat which once fed a water mill; it will be an odd lane where there is nothing to be learned.

Every rock standing by the roadside is not the remnant of a cross base, but if it lies beside an old route at a high point in the track where the site also coincides with an ancient boundary it might just be one. There is also the distinct possibility of cross remnants turning up in unexpected places, if the Shallcross could be discovered in a garden why not others?

When you next see an ancient sculpted cross, pause for a moment and think of the skill and patience required for its making and also what it must have looked like when it was newly carved and painted in bright colours.

I hope this book encourages others to keep a look out for antiquities, after all they are a part of our history. Ancient crosses are not confined to the Peak and fine examples can be found throughout the British Isles, but as Rev G.F. Browne pointed out, no other nation in Europe has such memorials. These examples of early Christian art should be as important to us as the Elgin Marbles are to the Greeks. As such, greater care should be taken with their preservation, perhaps by moving them inside churches as at Ecclesfield or Bradfield to save them from the corrosive effects of acid rain, or if they are to continue in their present positions, consideration should be given to giving the best of them some protective coating.

This survey has discovered several examples of wayside crosses being removed and placed in gardens or private collections. Whilst the legality of such actions may be suspect, it is I think better that antiquities be preserved in this manner rather than destroyed or lost. All I ask is that a proper record be kept of where they stood originally and that access be available to those with a genuine interest.

ACKNOWLEDGEMENTS

I cannot finish without acknowledging the pioneering work done by G.H.B. Ward and the Rev. Charles Cox, and Rev. G.F. Browne. These worthy gentlemen started the ball rolling and committed their findings to paper, thus giving others a foundation on which to build. After Rev. Cox's tremendous outpouring of work on Derbyshire churches and history one can only marvel as to where he found the time to go seeking crosses in remote spots. Rev. Cox cast doubts on historian Llewellynn Jewitt's ideas and Ward in his turn found errors in Cox's work. G.H.B. Ward spent much of his spare time walking over the countryside in question, talking to farmers, gamekeepers and local folks, and also spent many hours thoroughly checking old documents in record offices and libraries. He also wrote dozens of interesting pieces in the Sheffield Clarion Ramblers handbooks for many years. His opinions are always worthy of serious consideration.

I may have cast doubts on some of their opinions as no doubt others will on mine in due course, but it is only by constant questioning that we can hope to arrive at something approaching the truth. Today we have many advantages; large scale maps on film which can be examined in Record Offices with the aid of a micro reader; the motor car to enable us to inspect several sites in a short time; the Internet which can bring a reply within hours; and of course all the writings of the above.

The help of the following ladies has proved invaluable when it seemed that some problem was insoluble. Kate Atkinson, Archivist with the National Trust at Lyme Hall; Julie Bunting, an extraordinarily knowledgeable local historian and journalist; Barbara Foster of the Derbyshire Archaeological Society; and Ann Hearle of the Marple Historical Society. As ever, a host of folks in Record Offices and Local Studies Libraries have unearthed those odd gems of information which were eluding me, or suggested an appropriate line of approach.

Finally and most important of all, those stalwarts, Iris Brown, Terry Howard, Barry Shaw, David Sissons and Jan Stetka who have helped in so many ways. Taking photographs and measuring the dimensions of crosses after tramping to out of the way spots, discovering old maps, photocopying material, pestering local historians and reluctant clergymen who for some reason that eludes me, thought that the cure of souls had a greater priority than my researches, digging into archives, suggesting other cross sites and possible reasons for their choice. I could never have managed without them.

Neville T Sharpe,
Perth, January 2002

BIBLIOGRAPHY

Victoria Histories of Cheshire, Derbyshire and Staffordshire.

Articles in the *The Peak Advertiser*, by Julie Bunting.

Across The Derbyshire Moors, G.H.B. Ward.

Sheffield Clarion Ramblers annual booklets.

Memorials of Old Derbyshire. by Rev. J. Charles Cox.

Early History of Stocksbridge.

The Athenaeum. Articles by Rev J. Charles Cox.

Anglo-Saxon England, Sir Frank Stenton.

Combs My Village, M. Bellhouse.

The Lost Woman's Cross In Combs Edge, M. Bellhouse.

Chapel-en-le-Frith, W.B. Bunting.

Journal of Derbyshire Archeological Society.

Histories published by many churches in the region.

The Round-Shafted Pre-Norman Crosses of the North Staffordshire Area, by T. Pape, North Staffs. Field Club 1945–47.

Peakland Roads and Trackways, by A.E, & E.M. Dodd, available from Landmark Publishing.

On the Pre-Norman Sculptured Stones of Derbyshire. by Rev. G.F. Browne.

Packmen, Carriers & Packhorse Roads, by David Hey, available from Landmark Publishing.

Windyway Cross, Ipstones Edsge (photograph by C.L.M. Porter)

INDEX

Ousley Cross (photograph by C.L.M. Porter)

At the time of going to press, it became apparent that a further group of crosses in the Ashbourne area were still extant.

At Mayfield, the churchyard contains two crosses, both medieval, one a churchyard cross and the other a wayside cross brought from near The Hermitage at SK14934507 in the 1840s.

In the 1960s, the Clifton Butter Cross existed outside the Cock Inn. It was plain, cylindrical and about 16ins high. It has since disappeared. Norbury churchyard cross existed outside the porch at SK12554238 in 1966 according to the National Archaeological Records Office but now the shaft appears to have been taken inside to the nave. Blore churchyard contains a square socket stone with chamfered upper edges, but the shaft is modern.

Blore Cross (photograph by C.L.M. Porter)